**Marianne Sägebrecht,** star of *Zuckerbaby (Sugar Baby), Out of Rosenheim (Bagdad Cafe),* and *Rosalie Goes Shopping,* was featured on the official poster of the 1990 Munich Film Festival. [Used with the kind permission of Eberhard Hauff, Director of the festival. Original photograph by Walter Kober.]

# WEST GERMAN CINEMA 1985-1990

## A Reference Handbook

by
Richard C. Helt
and
Marie E. Helt

The Scarecrow Press, Inc.
Metuchen, N.J., & London
1992

British Library Cataloguing-in-Publication data available

Library of Congress Cataloging-in-Publication Data

Helt, Richard C.
   West German cinema, 1985-1990 : a reference handbook / by Richard
C. Helt and Marie E. Helt.
      p.   cm.
   Includes bibliographical references and indexes.
   Filmography: p.
   ISBN 0-8108-2647-X (acid-free paper)
   1. Motion pictures--Germany (West)--Handbooks, manuals, etc.
I. Helt, Marie E.   II. Title.
PN1993.5.G3H426  1992
791.43'0943--dc20                                            92-39433

**In Memoriam**

**Ulf Miehe**
(1940 - 1989)

Poet, novelist, filmmaker, friend

# CONTENTS

Preface — vii

Introduction — ix

Filmography — 1

Biographies - Directors — 187

Index of Directors — 199

Index of Actors and Actresses — 209

Cross-Reference Index of
    English Titles — 249

About the Authors — 259

## PREFACE

This reference work augments our original volume, *West German Cinema Since 1945: A Reference Handbook* (Scarecrow Press, 1987), and provides basic information about West German films right up to the first national election held in unified Germany in December, 1990.

While the gathering of information for this type of book is a continuing process, we are indebted to three very reliable sources, the *Lexikon des internationalen Films* (Rowohlt Verlag, Hamburg, which succeeds the *Handbücher der katholischen Filmkritik*), *Kino* (the annual distribution catalogue of the *Export-Union des deutschen Films* in Munich), and the excellent German cinema journal, *epd Film* (*Gemeinschaftswerk der Evangelischen Publizistik*, Frankfurt). Our research has also been informed by recent secondary works on German cinema, including the following, in English:

Elsaesser, Thomas. *New German Cinema: A History*. New Brunswick, N. J.: Rutgers University Press, 1989.

Kaes, Anton. *From Hitler to Heimat: The Return of History as Film*. Cambridge, MA: Harvard University Press, 1989.

McCormick, Richard W. *Politics of the Self: Feminism and the Postmodern in West German Literature and Film*. Princeton, N. J.: Princeton University Press, 1991.

Pflaum, Hans Günther. *Germany on Film: Theme and Content in the Cinema of the Federal Republic of Germany*. (Translated by Richard C. Helt and Roland Richter). Detroit, MI: Wayne State University Press, 1990.

Rentschler, Eric. *West German Filmmakers on Film: Visions and Voices.* New York: Holmes and Meier, 1988.

Many individuals, colleagues, and friends assisted us as we collected material and viewed films during our many stays in Germany, and those in Munich deserve special mention: Angelika Miehe, Günther Pflaum, Gisela Freudenberg, and Elisabeth and Peter Hoffmann. A note of thanks must also go to Eberhard Hauff, director of the Munich Film Festival, for regularly providing us with information, material, and passes for the festival!

The authors also express sincere gratitude to Henry Hooper, Associate Vice President for Academic Affairs at Northern Arizona University, and Karl Webb, former Dean of the College of Arts and Sciences here, for providing generous financial support that allowed us to complete our research in Germany during the summer of 1992. For their patient and competent technical assistance, we also thank the staff of Bilby Research Center at Northern Arizona University.

Richard C. Helt          Flagstaff, Arizona
Marie E. Helt          October 20, 1992

# INTRODUCTION

When we were completing our original volume of this work during the fall of 1986, we were already collecting material--and viewing films--for a supplement which was to be published in 1995 and was to cover the next ten years of West German cinematic production after the publication of *West German Cinema Since 1945: A Reference Handbook*. Obviously, the events of 1989 in Germany made it necessary for us to change those plans!

As regular visitors to Germany, we were perhaps less surprised than some at the demise of the German Democratic Republic, but we admit to being amazed at the rapidity with which that country was, in effect, annexed (democratically and legally, to be sure!) by the Federal Republic of Germany. As the initial elation began to wear off, we saw that among the myriad changes that were occurring in Germany there would inevitably be significant developments within the film cultures of the GDR and the FRG as the two nations merged. Indeed, the realization came quickly that these two national cinemas, which had existed side by side--yet distinctly separate--for more than forty years, would no longer exist. We thus decided to compose this supplement to our original work, in effect closing the "chapter" of film history entitled *West German Cinema*.

Since our first volume provides a brief history of German cinema from its beginning in 1895 up to 1985, we felt that a recounting of the past five years of West German cinematic history would be less informative--especially as regards the future direction of *German* cinema--than an interview with a critic who is among those most knowledgeable about West German cinema.

Hans Günther Pflaum is the author of numerous books, articles, and reviews of German and world cinema, and he contributes regularly to Munich's *Süddeutsche Zeitung*, to *epd Film*, as well as to radio and television. In 1992, he produced a two-hour

television retrospective on Rainer Werner Fassbinder on the tenth
anniverary of the renowned director's death. During our 1991-92
sabbatical in Marbach am Neckar, we had several opportunities to
meet with him in Munich. The following interview, begun during the
Munich Film Festival in early July, 1992, was edited and enlarged by
Hans Günther Pflaum in September, 1992, and translated by the
authors.

[**RCH** = Richard C. Helt; **HGP** = Hans Günther Pflaum]

**RCH:** What do you see as particularly positive and encouraging
developments in West German cinema during the years 1945 to 1990?

**HGP:** The most positive development in the cinema of the Federal
Republic between 1945 and 1990 would have to be the emergence of
the New German Cinema movement in the sixties with its attempt to
break irrevocably with the filmmaking of the older generation and its
traditions. A couple of directors have to be mentioned, without
whom this break with the past would have been unthinkable:
Alexander Kluge, the French immigrant Jean-Marie Straub, Vlado
Kristl (with his anarchistic camera style), the experimental filmmaker
Werner Nekes, and, of course, the second generation of the New
German Cinema, Rainer Werner Fassbinder and Wim Wenders.
Werner Herzog should be mentioned, too, along with the young
Volker Schlöndorff.

It can definitely be said that there were some unmistakably
distinctive styles among that group of German directors. Now,
though, I'd say that Herbert Achternbusch is the only German
director with a distinct, unmistakably personal style. Our film
schools, the various forms of film subsidies, and television have
increasingly influenced German filmmaking and served to "channel"
it in a single direction.

**RCH:** What were the weaknesses of West German cinema, and why,
in your opinion, was it not successful in capturing more than only a
modest share of even the German movie market?

**HGP:** The main weakness of West German cinema was, for some,
actually its major strength: Often the head dominated over the heart
in these films, which gave them an intellectual appeal but made

communication with a broader audience difficult. More decisive in the eventual failure of German cinema to establish itself, though, was the belief that only with big money, i. e., only by adopting budget and production standards of international magnitude, could one produce good and successful films. However, not a single director in the New German Cinema movement could say that his or her best film was also the most expensive one.

It was the belief in the necessity of more and more money that eventually delivered most German filmmakers into the hands of the various subsidy commissions (which, by the way, are dominated and controlled by political forces), at the same time making them dependent upon television. Only in this manner could the conservative political shift of the eighties make its influence felt in the production of cinema in Germany, too.

These developments have also contributed to the loss of a share of the movie market. The German cinema industry is a colony of Hollywood, a fact that has to do with developments in Germany in the immediate post-WW II period, as well as with the age-old dream of many German directors to succeed in Hollywood. Any attempt, however, to beat Hollywood at its own game is based purely on delusions of grandeur; only the rarest of Hollywood-style German films succeeds commercially.

**RCH:** Did West German cinema distinguish itself in any particular way during its "final" years, 1985-90? What films of this period do you consider worthy of mention?

**HGP:** West German cinema of that period is characterized, with few exceptions, by its aesthetic uniformity; the distinctive, individualized directorial styles of earlier years seem to have conformed to a kind of "normality." Some exceptions: the films of Herbert Achternbusch, as mentioned above, especially *Niemandsland (No Man's Land)* and *I know the Way to the Hofbräuhaus;* Werner Schroeter (*Malina*); Wim Wenders's *Der Himmel über Berlin (Wings of Desire)*, and Edgar Reitz's new *Heimat 2 (Homeland 2)*, though it is conceived as a television series and is many hours longer than the original *Heimat.*

**RCH:** Although we in the West (especially in North America) know relatively little about the cinema of the former German Democratic

Republic, there was an active filmmaking community there that, despite considerable difficulties, made some good films. While many of the negative aspects of the GDR's film production system are obvious, were there noteworthy positive characteristics of that film industry?

**HGP:** There were three clear accomplishments of the East German film production agency, DEFA [*Deutsche Filmaktiengesellschaft*]. First and foremost, they set as a top priority--from the very beginning--the task of coming to grips with German fascism. While West German cinema reestablished itself after the war with light-weight entertainment, DEFA's first production was Wolfgang Staudte's *Die Mörder sind unter uns (The Murderers Are Among Us)*. The East's second achievement was in the area of the documentary film, and in this genre, too, the DEFA could be viewed as exemplary. Finally, there was a whole series of wonderful children's films that had not the slightest tinge of ideological indoctrination.

**RCH:** What GDR directors and which films do you consider particularly worthy of mention or, indeed, of recommendation?

**HGP:** The most important filmmakers of the GDR would have to include: Konrad Wolf and his entire oeuvre, especially his films *Sterne (Stars), Lissy, Sonnensucher (Sun Seekers), Ich war neunzehn (I Was Nineteen)*, and *Solo Sunny;* Frank Beyer (whose *Spur der Steine (Trail of Stones)* was perhaps the best DEFA feature film of all!) with *Fünf Patronenhülsen (Five Empty Shells), Jakob der Lügner (Jacob the Liar)*, and *Geschlossene Gesellschaft (Private Party);* Egon Günther, *Die Schlüssel (The Keys)* and *Der Dritte (The Third Man)*.
　　　　Among the documentary filmmakers, I would select Jürgen Böttcher for, among other works, *Ofenbauer (Oven Builders), Der Sekretär (The Secretary), Wäscherinnen (Washer Women)* and Volker Koepp for *Mädchen in Wittstock (Girls in Wittstock), Wieder in Wittstock (Back in Wittstock)*, and *Das weite Feld (That Covers a Lot)*.

**RCH:** It's been nearly two years since the unification of Germany. Is it possible yet to speak in any sense of a unification of German cinema or, at least, of an "integration" of the East German film industry into that of the West?

**HGP:** As of today, you cannot speak of an integration of the film industry of the former GDR (which, of course, was basically not an "industry" anyway!) into the West German cinema industry - the overall cinema situation is, after all, much too difficult for that to be possible. The various film subsidy commissions have been very considerate of filmmakers in the new federal states [i. e., those in the territory of the former GDR], but there are very few directors who have been able to continue making films without interruption during the process of unification. An exception would be the above mentioned Frank Beyer, though he had already occasionally worked in the West in earlier years. In essence, this means that many ex-GDR directors are not doing as well today, financially, as they were before unification, but they are not doing any worse than many other filmmakers in the Federal Republic have been doing for years. The most regrettable thing is that documentary filmmakers from the former GDR will only be able to survive by working in television.

Those, on the other hand, who are already achieving a kind of integration are the actors and actresses from the former GDR, at least those who had already really established themselves there.

**RCH:** The purchase of the DEFA by the French company CGE (Compagnie Générale des Eaux) has been completed. While one of the most important figures in West German cinema, Volker Schlöndorff, enthusiastically supported the French, other film people in the West--and especially, it is said, in Munich--were against the sale. How do you view this deal?

**HGP:** I am actually quite skeptical about this deal, because I have believed from the start that the purchasers were not primarily interested in preserving any particular cinema tradition, but rather in acquiring the real estate on which the DEFA-UFA studios in Berlin are located. On the other hand, though, this purchase was probably the only economically justifiable solution, especially in view of the fact that no interested party within Germany had that kind of financial power. Without the intervention of the CGE, the Babelsberg studios in Potsdam, at least, would have eventually fallen into the hands of real estate speculators. Still, the fear persists that CGE may not be interested in the continuation of filmmaking there.

Volker Schlöndorff, though, is of a different opinion. As far as he's concerned, Babelsberg is "a name as good as Hollywood" - as a flyer in my press packet at the recent Venice Film Festival proclaimed!

**RCH:** At a press conference during this year's Cannes festival, Wim Wenders proposed that the number of Hollywood films imported into Europe should be limited, and he even suggested that particularly violent films should not be allowed into Europe at all. While few film people in Europe would share such an extreme position, many cling to the hope of establishing a European film industry that would be able to compete with Hollywood, at least on the continent. What's your opinion about that?

**HGP:** The German film industry will never be able to compete with Hollywood; indeed, even attempting to compete will only weaken it. The future of German cinema, if there is one at all, lies in returning to the virtues and strengths of the *auteur* film, its imagination and its intellect. German cinema can never achieve the perfection of Hollywood cinema, nor will it ever be able to approximate the economic power of Hollywood. It should be the goal of all European national cinemas to build up a market--at least on the European continent--that is large enough to allow individual productions to free themselves somewhat from their present dependence upon subsidy commissions. But then, who in Germany is interested, for example, in a Portuguese film - or who in Portugal in a German movie?

At any rate, competition with Hollywood, or with any form of American cinema at all, would only be sensible in the realm of the low-budget movie. Major European productions, such as *Der Name der Rose (The Name of the Rose)*, succeed only in the rarest of cases on the world market. I don't expect that the establishment of the new European market system will change that, at least not in the foreseeable future.

# FILMOGRAPHY OF WEST GERMAN CINEMA 1985 - 1990

The following filmography contains all West German feature films made between 1985 and 1990, including co-productions with directors from other countries. Most films that are not commercially distributed, such as those produced only for television broadcast and thus little known outside of the Federal Republic, as well as documentary and educational films, are not included here.

For many English titles the authors have relied primarily on listings in *Kino*, the annual catalogue of the *Export-Union des deutschen Films* in Munich. All other titles are the authors' own translations.

**Format of filmography entries:**

> **Year of production** - co-productions with other countries noted in parentheses
> **Titles** - in alphabetical order by German title, English title in parentheses
> **Synopsis of content**
> **Dir.** - Director
> **SP.** - Screenplay author
> **Cam.** - Camera person
> **Mus.** - Composer of musical score
> **Prod.** - Producer
> **Act.** - Principal actors/actresses
> **Length of film in minutes**

## 1987 A.D.A.M.

Instead of showing up for his wedding, a dedicated archaeologist goes out to a sandy ditch where the skull of a primitive man has reportedly been discovered.

Dir.: Herbert Ballmann.
SP.: Hartmann Schmige.
Cam.: Ingo Hamer.
Mus.: Günther Fischer.
Prod.: Neue Filmproduktion TV.
Act.: Desiree Becker (Nosbusch), Helmut Berger, Yolande Gilot, Gunther Berger, Dirk Dautzenberg.
98 min.

## 1987-88 (English-Italian-German) *Die Abenteuer des Baron Münchhausen* (*The Adventures of Baron Munchhausen*)

Remake of the fantastic experiences of Karl Friedrich Freiherr von Münchhausen.

Dir.: Terry Gilliam.
SP.: Charles McKeown, Terry Gilliam.
Cam.: Giuseppe Rotunno.
Mus.: Michael Kamen.
Prod.: Prominent Features/Laura/Thomas Schüly.
Act.: John Neville, Eric Idle, Sarah Polley Reed, Jonathan Pryce, Oliver Reed.
120 min.

## 1986 (USA-German) *Abenteuer im Spielzeugland* (*Babes in Toyland*)

An eleven-year-old girl dreams of a toyland, where she enjoys many adventures and fights the villain.

Dir.:   Clive Donner.
SP.:   Paul Zindel, Leslie Bricusse.
Cam.:   Arthur Ibbetson.
Mus.:   Leslie Bricusse.
Prod.:   The Finnegan Group/Bavaria.
Act.:   Drew Barrymore, Pat Morita, Richard Mulligan, Eileen Brennan, Keanu Reeves.
95 min.

1989 *Abrahams Gold (Abraham's Gold)*

A former concentration camp guard intends to realize his dreams of wealth and happiness by getting a friend to help him dig up a stash of gold he buried in Poland during the war.

Dir.:   Jörg Graser.
SP.:   Jörg Graser.
Cam.:   Hennig Stegmüller.
Prod.:   Avista/Pro-ject/Adamos Film/ZDF.
Act.:   Hanna Schygulla, Günther-Maria Halmer, Daniela Schötz, Robert Dietl, Maria Singer.
95 min.

1988 *Abschied vom falschen Paradies (Farewell to a False Paradise)*

A young Turkish woman, in German prison for killing her husband, finds solidarity with the women there. When she is released for good behaviour, she is threatened with deportation.

Dir.:   Tevfik Baser.
SP.:   Tevfik Baser, based on a novel by Salina Scheinhardt.
Cam.:   Izzet Akay.
Mus.:   Claus Bantzer.
Prod.:   Ottokar Runze Filmprod./ZDF.
Act.:   Zuhal Olcay, Brigitte Janner, Ruth Olafsdottir,

Barbara Morawiecz, Ayse Altan.
96 min.

## 1990 *Der achte Tag* *(The Eighth Day)*

A dedicated female journalist investigates a scientist's alleged suicide, and discovers a group of criminal gene "manipulators" who regard human life only as a research tool.

Dir.:     Reinhard Münster.
SP.:      Reinhard Münster.
Cam.:     Axel Block.
Mus.:     Günther Fischer.
Prod.:    Von Vietinghoff/WDR.
Act.:     Katharina   Thalbach,   Hans-Christian   Blech,
          Hannelore Elsner, Ulrich Pleitgen, Heinz Hoenig.
99 min.

## 1985 (German-Austrian) '38 - *Heim ins Reich* (*1938: Home to the Realm*)

After German troops march into Vienna in March 1938, a Jewish author falls into the hands of the Gestapo, while his pregnant girlfriend manages to escape to Prague.

Dir.:     Wolfgang Glück.
SP.:      Wolfgang Glück, from a novel by Friedrich
          Torberg.
Cam.:     Gerard Vandenberg.
Mus.:     Bert Gund.
Prod.:    Satel/Almaro/ORF/BR.
Act.:     Tobias Engel, Sunnyi Melles, Heinz Trixner, Lotte
          Ledl, Ingrid Burkhard.
97 min.

## 1987 *Adrian und die Römer* (*Adrian and the Romans*)

A forty-year-old man suffers an identity crisis and skids from one adventure to another, until he meets up with an old girlfriend and her daughter and finds himself.

> Dir.:    Klaus Bueb, Thomas Mauch.
> SP.:     Klaus Bueb.
> Cam.:    Thomas Mauch.
> Mus.:    Claus Bantzer.
> Prod.:   Ottokar Runze Filmprod.
> Act.:    Klaus Bueb, Gertraud Jesserer, Katharina Abt,
>          Sabine von Maydell, Hark Bohm.
> 93 min.

1989  (German-French)  *African Timber*

A young German manager is sent to a rundown sawmill in Ghana,
where he discovers a thriving smuggling operation of valuable tropical
wood.

> Dir.:    Peter F. Bringmann.
> SP.:     Christoph Mattner.
> Cam.:    Frank Brühne.
> Mus.:    Paul Vincent Gunnia.
> Prod.:   Neue Deutsche Film/WDR/Project/Torii.
> Act.:    Heiner Lauterbach, Julien Guiomar, Deborah
>          Lacey, Dietmar Schönherr, Kofi Baba Bucknor.
> 99 min.

1985  *AIDS - Die schleichende Gefahr (AIDS - The Coming Danger)*

Four episodes depict various victims of AIDS.

> Dir/SP.: Peter Grandl.
> Cam.:    Siegfried Krauss.
> Mus.:    Harry Wing, Buddy J. Raindom.
> Prod.:   Galerie Film/Diva Film & Musik Prod.
> Act.:    Birgit Winter, Nina Cronjäger, Frank Garbo, Monic
>          Creip, Johannes Jecloos.
> 86 min.

1985  *Alphacity - Abgerechnet wird nachts (Alphacity)*

Two men fight for the love of a woman in the night world of Berlin's
bars and discotheques.

Dir/SP.:  Eckhart Schmidt.
Cam.:     Bernd Neubauer.
Mus.:     Fox Mountain.
Prod.:    Starfilm/Extrafilm/Neue Tele-Contact.
Act.:     Al Corley, Isabelle Gutzwiller, Claude Oliver
          Rudolph, Jürgen Draeger, Peter von Strombeck.
101 min.

### 1984 *Amerasia (Amerasia)*

A black Vietnam veteran searches for himself and for a sense of
belonging to his American homeland. He goes to Bangkok to apply
for an entrance visa for Vietnam, and there he is confronted by GIs
who stayed behind and thousands of Amerasian children there.

Dir.:     Wolf-Eckart Bühler.
SP.:      Wolf-Eckart Bühler.
Cam.:     Bernd Fiedler.
Mus.:     Terry Allen.
Prod.:    Red Harvest Film.
Act.:     John Anderson, Gillian Tuyudee Hornett, Surachai
          Jantimatorn, Terry Allen, Paijong Laisakul.
97 min.

### 1989 *American Beauty Ltd.*

A film with several episodes, which tell the stories of various
immigrants and workers in America.

Dir.:     Dieter Marcello.
SP.:      Dieter Marcello.
Cam.:     Axel Block.
Mus.:     Wolfgang Hamm.
Prod.:    Dieter Marcello project + film.
Act.:     Liora Hilb, Walter Sachers.
89 min.

1985 *André schafft sie alle (Girls' Favorite Sport)*

André, who runs a karate school in Vienna, surmounts life's economic obstacles by having beautiful women work for him.

Dir.: Peter Fratzscher.
SP.: Josef Ebner.
Cam.: Bernd Heinl.
Prod.: Avisia-Film/SplendidFilmProd./Pro-JectFilmprod.
Act.: Franco Nero, Ingrid Steeger, Dolores Schmidinger.
92 min.

1986 *Der Angriff (The Attack)*

An attorney's wife is the victim of a sexual attack by two juveniles.

Dir.: Theodor Kotulla.
SP.: Theodor Kotulla.
Cam.: Jacques Steyn.
Mus.: Eberhard Weber.
Prod.: Iduna.
Act.: Pascale Petit, Michael König, Claude-Oliver Rudolph, Andras Fricsay, Lambert Hamel.
120 min.

1985 *Der Angriff der Gegenwart auf die übrige Zeit (The Present Attacks the Rest of Time)*

A filmic "essay," consisting of numerous episodes and sketches, about the phenomenon of time and about the cinema medium. (Partly black/white.)

Dir/SP.: Alexander Kluge.
Cam.: Thomas Mauch, Werner Lüring, Herrmann Fahr, Judith Kaufmann.
Act.: Jutta Hoffmann, Armin Mueller-Stahl, Michael Rehberg, Peter Roggisch, Rosel Zech.
113 min.

## 1987 *Anita - Tänze des Lasters  (Anita - Dances of Vice)*

An elderly lady swears that she was one of the greatest dancers of the
silent film era, but her story turns out to be pure fantasy.

| | |
|---|---|
| Dir.: | Rosa von Praunheim. |
| SP.: | Hannelene Limpach, Rosa von Praunheim, Marianne Enzensberger, Lotti Huber. |
| Cam.: | Elfi Mikesch. |
| Mus.: | Konrad Elfers, Rainer Rubbert, Alan Marks, Ed Lieber. |
| Prod.: | Rosa von Praunheim Filmprod./Road Movies/ZDF. |
| Act.: | Lotti Huber, Ina Blum, Mikael Honesseau, Tillmann Lehnert, Marion Kutschke. |
| 85 min. | |

## 1988 *Anna*

A young female dancer gets the opportunity to advance her ballet
career in Munich and New York, but this causes problems in her
relationship with her wheelchair-bound boyfriend.

| | |
|---|---|
| Dir.: | Frank Strecker. |
| SP.: | Justus Pfaue. |
| Cam.: | Peter Ambach. |
| Mus.: | Gisi Schwab. |
| Prod.: | TV-60/ZDF. |
| Act.: | Silvia Seidel, Patrick Bach, Jan Peterson, Eberhard Feik, Ilse Neubauer. |
| 95 min. | |

## 1987-89 (German-Swiss) *Der Atem  (The Spirit)*

The murderer of a young girl is still living in her family's
neighborhood twenty years later.

| | |
|---|---|
| Dir.: | Niklaus Schilling. |
| SP.: | Niklaus Schilling. |
| Cam.: | Bernd Neubauer, Thomas Meyer. |

Mus.: Georges Delerue, Francis Lai, Vladimir Cosma, Paul Guiot, Michael Rüggenberg.
Prod.: Elke Haltaufderheide.
Act.: Charles Brauer, Ian Moorse, Karina Fallenstein, Ankie Beilke, Franz Boehm, Liane Hielscher; Sabine Trooger, Sunnyi Melles.
119 min.

1987 *Ätherrausch* (*Ether Delirium*)

At an international electronics company, research is being done in the area of consciousness expansion through electronics; the research department chair soon finds that he is the subject of industrial espionage.

Dir.: Klaus Gengnagel.
SP.: Klaus Gengnagel.
Cam.: Mike Bartlett.
Mus.: Kristian Schultze.
Prod.: Senso Film/BR/HR.
Act.: Klaus Grünberg, Sabine Dornblut, Rudolf Schündler, Franz Wismuth, Remus Muntean.
97 min.

1985 *Auf immer und ewig* (*For Ever and Ever*)

A woman living alone with her young son learns that she has a terminal disease. She decides to try to get back together with the boy's father, and once she rediscovers love, she is ready to deal with her life-threatening operation.

Dir.: Christel Buschmann.
SP.: Christel Buschmann.
Cam.: Frank Brühne.
Mus.: Chris Rea.
Prod.: Rocco/ZDF.
Act.: Eva Mattes, Werner Stocker, Theo Gostischa, Silke Wülfing, August Zirner.
97 min.

1987   (French-German)   *Auf Wiedersehen, Kinder   (Good-bye Children)*

In a Catholic boarding school in the winter of 1944, a 12-year-old French boy befriends one of three Jewish boys who are being hidden at the school. Their friendship ends brutally when the Gestapo discovers the deception.

> Dir.:   Louis Malle.
> SP.:    Louis Malle.
> Cam.:   Renato Berta.
> Mus.:   Franz Schubert, Camille Saint-Saens.
> Prod.:  NEF/Stella/Nouvelles Editions de Films/M.K.2/Centre National du Cinema/Investimages/Sofia Creations.
> Act.:   Gaspard Manesse, Raphael Fejtö, Francine Racette, Philippe Morier-Genoud, Francois Negret.
> 105 min.

1987   *Aufbrüche   (Awakenings)*

A seventeen-year-old Turkish girl is to be married to a Turkish man without her say. She leaves home, finds a place in a youth home, and begins training to become a photographer. But her father, whose honor is being threatened, kidnaps her and finds another husband for her in Munich.

> Dir.:   Hartmut Horst, Eckart Lottmann.
> SP.:    Hartmut Horst, Eckart Lottmann.
> Cam.:   Kenan Ormanlar.
> Mus.:   Tayfun.
> Prod.:  Medien Operative.
> Act.:   Deniz Seyhun, Tuncel Kurtiz, Özay Fecht, Ilona Lawanowski, Nina Schultz.
> 89 min.

1987  (German-USA)   *Ein Aufstand alter Männer   (A Gathering of Old Men)*

When a white farmer in Louisiana is shot by a black man, a group of eighteen elderly black men bands together, and each one claims to have done the deed. Through their solidarity, they overcome their fear.

Dir.: Volker Schlöndorff.
SP.: Charles Fuller, from a novel by Ernest J. Gaines.
Cam.: Edward Lachman.
Mus.: Ron Carter.
Prod.: Consolidated/Jennie & Co./Zenith/Bioskop/HR.
Act.: Louis Gossett, Jr., Richard Widmark, Holly Hunter, Joe Seneca, Will Patton.
91 min.

1984-85 *Ausgeträumt (Holiday)*

A young lathe operator is bored with his monotonous work and decides to go off to Munich to a pop music concert. When his car breaks down on the way, he meets up with a group of cabaret artists and ends up joining them, becoming politically active, and participating in a peace demonstration for which he is jailed.

Dir.: Hajo Baumgärtner.
SP.: Hajo Baumgärtner.
Cam.: Lennart Kremser.
Mus.: Andreas Bung.
Prod.: Hajo Baumgärtner Prod.
Act.: Kai Dette, Ursula Buchfellner, Ilja Richter, Die kleine Tierschau.
102 min.

## 1986 *Ballhaus Barmbek - Let's kiss and say goodbye*

The scene is a ballroom in Barmbek where lonely people can come and meet other lonely people and dance together.

Dir.: Christel Buschmann.
SP.: Christel Buschmann.
Cam.: Mike Gast.
Mus.: Various pop artists.
Prod.: Roxy-Film.
Act.: Jörg Pfennigwerth, Ulrich Tukur, Kiev Stingl, Zazie de Paris, Nico.
80 min.

## 1981 *Bananen Paul (Banana Paul)*

When a bear escapes the circus in a sleepy little town, it causes an uproar. But the beast turns out to be quite harmless, befriends a young girl, and embarks on a number of adventures with her.

Dir.: Richard Claus.
SP.: Richard Claus, Manfred Weis.
Cam.: Jörg Geshel.
Mus.: Piet Klocke.
Prod.: C & H Film/ZDF.
Act.: May Buschke, Otto Schnelling, Martin Lüttge, Gunter Berger, Marcel Werner.
84 min.

## 1989 *Bavaria Blue*

A German-born director travels through Bavaria for an American television station in order to research Bavarian folk music for a live

13

show that will be broadcast directly to America. He comes into contact with a wide variety of people and music types.

Dir.: Jörg Bundschuh.
SP.: Jörg Bundschuh.
Cam.: Jörg Schmidt-Reitwein.
Mus.: Haindling.
Prod.: Kick-Film.
Act.: Alfred Edel, Herbert Fux, Andy Geer, Sigmund Reindl, Juliette Marischa.
82 min.

1984 (German-French) *Beethoven*

The film concentrates on Beethoven's problematical relationship with his nephew, Karl, for whom he was legal guardian.

Dir.: Paul Morrissey.
SP.: Paul Morrissey, Mathieu Carriere, from a novel by Luigi Magnani.
Cam.: Hanus Polak.
Mus.: Ludwig van Beethoven.
Prod.: CBL/Orfilm.
Act.: Wolfgang Reichmann, Dietmar Prinz, Jane Birkin, Matthieu Carriere, Nathalie Baye.
101 min.

1990 *Bei mir liegen Sie richtig (Non-Stop Trouble in the Hospital)*

The night security guard in a psychiatric clinic is caught stealing human organs, but is bribed into pretending to be a doctor to help cover up the criminal acts of others at the clinic.

Dir.: Ulrich Stark.
SP.: Wolfgang Limmer.
Cam.: Manfred Ensinger.
Mus.: Birger Heymann.
Prod.: UFA/ZDF.
Act.: Dieter Hallervorden, Rosel Zech, Ezard

Haußmann, Alexander May, Dieter Pfaff.
91 min.

## 1988 *Beim nächsten Mann wird alles anders* *(The Next Guy will be Different)*

Story of a young female film student in search of her dream man.
Comedy.

Dir.:   Xaver Schwarzenberger.
SP.:    Stefan Lukschy, Gundolf S. Freyermuth, from a novel by Eva Heller.
Cam.:   Xaver Schwarzenberger.
Mus.:   Hits of the 50s.
Prod.:  Rialto.
Act.:   Antje Schmidt, Volkert Kraeft, Dominic Raacke, Despina Pajanou, Billie Zöckler.
101 min.

## 1986 *Bibo's Männer* *(Bibo's Men)*

A self-confident but brusque young woman has trouble getting along with anyone, but finally finds love in the big city.

Dir.:   Klaus Lemke.
SP.:    Klaus Lemke.
Cam.:   Martin Schäfer.
Mus.:   Michael Landau.
Prod.:  Klaus Lemke/KF-Kinofilm/BR.
Act.:   Tanja Moravsky, Nikolaus Vogel, Dominic Raacke, Andy Kistner, Emel Wahl.
80 min.

## 1985 *Big Mäc (Big Mac)*

An out-of-work teacher takes part in a motorcycle rally, wins the race, and finds the woman of his dreams.

Dir.:   Sigi Rothemund.

Cam.:    Frank Brühne.
Mus.:    Robert Pferdmenges.
Act.:    Thomas Gottschalk, Beate Finckh, Ankie Beilke,
         Eiji Kusuhara, Loni von Friedl.
86 min.

1986  *Bitte laßt die Blumen leben  (Please Let the Flowers Live)*

Following a plane crash, a Parisian lawyer builds a new identity for
himself with falsified documents, in order to escape his mid-life crisis.

Dir.:    Duccio Tessari.
SP.:     Joachim Hammann, from a novel by Johannes
         Mario Simmel.
Cam.:    Charly Steinberger.
Mus.:    Frank Duval.
Prod.:   Roxy/Lisa/Ilse KubaschewskiFilmproduktion/BR.
Act.:    Klaus-Jürgen Wussow, Birgitt Doll, Hannelore
         Elsner, Hans-Christian Blech, Radost Bokel.
99 min.

1988-89  *Blauäugig  (Blue-eyed)*

Decades after his parents had been taken away by the SS, a German-
Czech emigrant, now living in Argentina as a weapons dealer,
becomes a victim of the same kind of state terror when troops from
a military junta kidnap and murder his daughter.

Dir.:    Reinhard Hauff.
SP.:     Dorothee Schön.
Cam.:    Hector Morini, Jaroslav Kucera.
Mus.:    Marcel Wengler.
Prod.:   Bioskop/ZDF.
Act.:    Götz George, Michel Angel Sola, Julio de Grazia,
         Alex Benn, Emilia Mazer.
87 min.

1986  (German-Argentinian)  *Ein Blick und die Liebe bricht aus*
*(One Look and It's Love)*

A film that reflects the many facets of the feminist debate, including exploitation of women, sexism, etc.

Dir.:   Jutta Brückner.
SP.:    Jutta Brückner.
Cam.:   Marcello Carmorino.
Mus.:   Brynmore L. Jones.
Prod.:  von Vietinghoff.
Act.:   Elida Araoz, Rosario Belfari, Regina Lamm, Margarita Munoz, Marie Elena Rivera.
86 min.

1987 *Blue Blood*

A woman witnesses a murder in Munich, then decides to go underground and hide out, but the murderer, a high society Frenchman, hires a group of killers to find her.

Dir.:   Robert W. Young.
SP.:    Brian Clemens.
Cam.:   Alex Clemens.
Prod.:  Tele-München Fernseh-GmbH.
Act.:   Albert Fortell, Capucine, Lauren Hutton, Ursula Karven, Friedrich von Thun.
92 min.

1985 *Blue Moon - Atemlos durch die Nacht (Blue Moon - Breathless Through the Night)*

A young woman comes from the provinces to visit Berlin, where she witnesses a murder. As she flees, she loses her purse, from which the murderers extract her address. She seeks refuge with her boyfriend, not knowing he is the leader of the band of murderers.

Dir.:   Karsten Wichniarz.
SP.:    Karsten Wichniarz, from a story by Joachim Hammann.
Cam.:   Wolfgang Pilgrim.
Mus.:   D. Moebius.

Prod.:   Tröster Film/Roxy.
Act.:    Birgit Anders, Jean J. Straub, Klaus Kelterborn,
         Günter Notthoff, Wolfgang Schumacher.
87 min.

1980-81 *Blut & Ehre - Jugend unter Hitler (Blood and Honor - Youth in Hitler's Realm)*

The experiences of enthusiastic Hitler Youth members from various social and political backgrounds in a small town during the years 1933 to 1939.

Dir.:    Bernd Fischerauer.
SP.:     Helmut Kissel, Robert Müller.
Cam.:    Hannes Hollmann, Fritz Stachowski.
Mus.:    Ernst Brandner.
Prod.:   SWF.
Act.:    Rolf Becker, Jeffrey Frank, Steffen Rübling, Marlies
         Engel, Gila von Weitershausen.
113 min.

1983 (German-Polish) *Blutiger Schnee (Zu Freiwild verdammt) (Ruth)*

In Poland, 1943, a young Jewish girl barely escapes being transported to a concentration camp, and then must remain in hiding.

Dir.:    Jerzy Hoffman.
SP.:     Jerzy Hoffman, Jan Purzycki, from a story by Art
         Bernd.
Cam.:    Jerzy Goscik.
Mus.:    Andrzej Korzynski.
Prod.:   CCC-Filmkunst/SFB/PRF Zespoly Filmowe Zespol
         "Zodiak".
Act.:    Sharon Brauner, Anna Dymna, Günther Lamprecht,
         Matthieu Carriere.
94 min.

## 1988 *Bodo*

A young boy who is a computer freak suffers the teasing of his fellow pupils as well as pressure from his superachiever parents. He uses a computer program to clone a replica of himself, which is also a superachiever.

Dir.: Gloria Behrens.
SP.: Christos Konstantin, H. H. Weber.
Cam.: Leo Borchard.
Mus.: Kambiz Giahi.
Prod.: Olga Film/ZDF.
Act.: Martin Forbes, Gary Forbes, Nascica Kukavica, Heiner Lauterbach, Ulrike Krieger.
96 min.

## 1987 *Born For Love*

A movie actress is supposed to give a screen test for a porno movie, but she has difficulties in this new genre.

Dir.: Sascha Alexander.
SP.: S. X. Kowalski.
Cam.: Hughes Baron.
Prod.: Teresa Orlowski Verlag.
Act.: Sibylle Rauch, John Leslie, Karin Schubert.
82 min.

## 1987-88 *Brennende Betten (Burning Beds)*

A Hamburg woman who wants to break out of her mold meets up with a charming Englishman, who just happens also to be a pyromaniac.

Dir.: Pia Frankenberg.
SP.: Pia Frankenberg.
Cam.: Raoul Coutard.
Mus.: Horst Mühlbradt.
Prod.: Pia Frankenberg Prod./Hamburger

Filmbüro/Hamburger Wirtschaftsfilmförderung.
Act.: Ian Dury, Pia Frankenberg, Gerhard Garbers,
Frances Tomelty, Jennifer Hibbert.
85 min.

1988 (German-English) *Brennendes Geheimnis (Burning Secret)*

The brief, passionate encounter between an Austrian Baron and the wife of an American diplomat destroys the spontaneous feelings of a twelve-year-old boy, who feels himself betrayed by the Baron.

Dir.: Andrew Birkin.
SP.: Andrew Birkin, from a story by Stefan Zweig.
Cam.: Ernest Day.
Mus.: Hans Zimmer.
Prod.: B.A./N.F.H./Vestron Pictures/BR.
Act.: Faye Dunaway, Klaus Maria Brandauer, David Eberts, Eva Roth, Martin Obernigg.
105 min.

1987 *Das Brot des Siegers oder Die Schlacht um die Mägen der Welt (The Victor's Spoils or The Battle for the Stomachs of the World)*

Using an American hamburger empire as an example, this film deals with the phenomenon of the fast-food "culture."

Dir.: Peter Heller.
SP.: Peter Heller.
Cam.: Otmar Schmid, Bernd Fiedler, Kevin Keating, etc.
Mus.: Andreas Köbner.
Prod.: Filmkraft.
Act.: Ron Williams.
110 min. (16 mm.)

1989 *Bumerang - Bumerang (Boomerang - Boomerang)*

A sixteen-year-old high school girl spontaneously kidnaps a politician who is dedicated to the development of nuclear energy resources and keeps him prisoner with the help of two friends.

Dir.: Hans W. Geissendörfer.
SP.: Irene Fischer, Dorothee Schön.
Cam.: Hans-Günther Bücking.
Mus.: Dennis Hart.
Prod.: Geissendörfer/WDR/Pro-ject.
Act.: Katja Studt, Jürgen Vogel, Jan Plewka, Lambert
Hamel, Bernd Tauber.
102 min.

1989 *Butterbrot (Bread and Butter)*

Three male friends in their mid-thirties reflect on their situation in life as well as their difficulties with love and profession.

Dir.: Gabriel Barylli.
SP.: Gabriel Barylli, from his play.
Cam.: Thomas Mauch.
Mus.: Harald Kloser.
Prod.: Bavaria/Iduna Film.
Act.: Uwe Ochsenknecht, Heinz Hoenig, Gabriel Barylli,
Tina Brauer, Natascha Aghfurian.
92 min.

1990  *Cafe Europa*

An incompetent policeman is transferred to duty at the main train station in Munich, where he accidentally learns of plans to murder the owner of the Cafe Europa. Comedy.

Dir.: Franz Xaver Bogner.
SP.: Ekkehard Ziedrich, Franz Xaver Bogner.
Cam.: Frank Brühne.
Mus.: Rainhard Fendrich.
Prod.: Roxy-Film.
Act.: Jacques Breuer, Barbara Auer, August Zirner, Elmar Wepper, Raimund Harmstorf.
91 min.

1989  *Carmen on Ice*

The well-known drama about jealousy, this time transposed to the medium of ice dance, with the music of Georges Bizet.

Dir.: Horant H. Hohlfeld.
SP.: Horant H. Hohlfeld.
Cam.: Klaus König.
Mus.: Georges Bizet, Bert Grund.
Prod.: Vegas Film.
Act.: Katarina Witt, Brian Boitano, Brian Orser, Yvonne Gomez, Otto Retzer.
86 min.

1986  *Caspar David Friedrich - Grenzen der Zeit  (Caspar David Friedrich - Limits of Time)*

This film interprets the works and life of the romantic painter as a prophet of ecological consciousness.

Dir.:   Peter Schamoni.
SP.:    Peter Schamoni, Hans A. Neunzig.
Cam.:   Gerard Vandenberg.
Mus.:   Hans Possegga, Motives by Franz Schubert.
Prod.:  Allianz/Peter Schamoni Filmprod./BR/Defa/Argos.
Act.:   Helmut Griem, Sabine Sinjen, Hans Peter
        Hallwachs, Walter Schmidinger, Hans Quest.
84 min.

1984 (English-German)  *Chinese Boxes*

A young American in Berlin gets entangled in a web of private
relationships and murderous deals with drug dealing and smuggling.

Dir.:   Christopher Petit.
SP.:    Christopher Petit, L.M. Kit Carson.
Cam.:   Peter Harvey.
Mus.:   Günther Fischer.
Prod.:  Palace Pictures/Chris Sievernich Prod.
Act.:   Will Patton, Gottfried John, Adelheid Arndt,
        Robbie Coltrane, Beate Jensen.
83 min.

1986 *Die Chinesen kommen  (The Chinese are Coming)*

An obsolete Bavarian machinery factory is to be dismantled and sold
to the Chinese, much to the chagrin of the four remaining factory
workers. But in the process of dismantling the factory, the workers
come to understand and like their Asian counterparts.

Dir.:   Manfred Stelzer.
SP.:    Ulrich Enzensberger, Manfred Stelzer.
Cam.:   David Slama.
Mus.:   Rio Reiser.
Prod.:  Journal Film/Maran Film/SDF.
Act.:   Jörg Hube, Hans Brenner, Martin Sperr, Monika
        Baumgartner, Rolf Zacher.

98 min.

1987 (French-German) *Chocolat - Verbotene Sehnsucht (Chocolate - Forbidden Desires)*

Cameroon, 1957: The lonely young wife of a French colonial official is attracted to her black butler.

Dir.:   Claire Denis.
SP.:    Claire Denis, Jean Pol Fargeau.
Cam.:   Robert Alazraki.
Mus.:   Abdullah Ibrahim.
Prod.:  Cinemanuel/MK 2/Cerito/Wim Wenders Prod./La Sept/Caroline Prod./Le FODIC/TF 1/WDR.
Act.:   Isaach de Bankole, Giulia Goschi, Cecile Ducasse, Mireille Perrier, Francois Cluzet.
105 min.

1987 *Cobra Verde*

A young cattle herder leaves the desert of Brazil to follow his dream of a better life. He becomes a bandit, a foreman of 600 black slaves, is deported to Africa as a slave dealer, and there is crowned as a deputy king.

Dir.:   Werner Herzog.
SP.:    Werner Herzog, from ideas from a novel by Bruce Chatwin.
Cam.:   Viktor Ruzika.
Mus.:   Popol Vuh.
Prod.:  Werner Herzog Film/ZDF.
Act.:   Klaus Kinski, King Ampaw, Jose Lewgoy, Salvatore Basile, Peter Berling.
111 min.

1987-88 (German-Italian) *Der Commander (The Commander)*

A commando is sent to the "Golden Triangle" in Indonesia to liquidate a drug dealer who is bribing his customers in Europe and

America.

> Dir.:    Anthony M. Dawson (=Antonio Margheriti).
> SP.:     Arne Elsholtz, Tito Carpi.
> Cam.:   Peter Baumgartner.
> Prod.:   Ascot/Prestige.
> Act.:    Lewis Collins, Lee van Cleef, Donald Pleasence, John Steiner, Manfred Lehmann.
> 104 min.

### 1985 *Cortuga (Parts I and II)*

A Hamburger fruit wholesaler takes over operations of his company in a banana republic, and his wife finds herself in support of the leftists in the impending revolution.

> Dir.:    Edwin Marian.
> Cam.:   Eberhard Geick.
> Prod.:   Horizont Filmproduktion.
> Act.:    Sissy Höfferer, Heiner Lauterbach, Friedrich Schütter, Angelique Duvier, Ludwig Haas.
> 180 min.

### 1986-87 *Crazy Boys*

A woman turns her emancipated idea of a male striptease troupe, the "Crazy Boys," into reality, in spite of several stumbling blocks.

> Dir.:    Peter Kern.
> SP.:     Peter Kern.
> Cam.:   Eberhard Geick.
> Mus.:   Franz Plasa.
> Prod.:   Horizont Film.
> Act.:    Barbara Fenner, Udo Schenk, Mechmet Yandirer, Margit Symo, Marianne Sägebrecht.
> 90 min.

1989  *Dana Lech*

Dana, a Polish woman, has been living in West Berlin for eight months and has burned all her bridges--until one day her past lover, Jan, knocks at the door.

Dir.:    Frank Guido Blasberg.
SP.:    Frank Guido Blasberg.
Cam.:    Stepan Benda.
Mus.:    Wolfgang Thiel.
Prod.:    Deutsche Film- und Fernsehakademie Berlin (DFFB).
Act.:    Brybida Mich, Pjotr Beluch, Mirella d'Angelo, René Hofschneider, Max Gertsch.
66 min.  (16 mm)

1988  (American-German)  *Dance Academy II*

A group from a dancing school in Los Angeles competes with a loosely organized group of dancing ruffians for scholarships and public financial support.

Dir.:    Ted Mather.
SP.:    Ted Mather, Ralph Engler.
Cam.:    Dennis Peters.
Mus.:    Guido de Angelis, Maurizio de Angelis, Ted Mather (Choreography).
Prod.:    T.P.I./Ascot.
Act.:    Sally Stewart, Carlos Gomez, Daniel Quinn, Christina Haack, Adrian Paul.
97 min.

1988 *Dandy*

An avant-garde version of Voltaire's "Candide".

Dir.:   Peter Sempel.
SP.:    Peter Sempel.
Cam.:   Frank Blasberg, Jonas Scholz, Norimichi Kasamatu,
        Peter Sempel.
Mus.:   "Einstürzende Neu-bauten", Nick Cave, Yello,
        Abwärts, Navajo Indians, Jessye Norman.
Prod.:  Niko Brücher/Peter Sempel.
Act.:   Blixa Bargeld, Nick Cave, Nina Hagen, Dieter
        Meier, Kazuo Ohno.
90 min.

1986 *Des Teufels Paradies* (*Devil's Paradise*)

A man seeks to escape civilization on an idyllic island, where an
intriguer finds pleasure in provoking him.

Dir.:   Vadim Glowna.
SP.:    Leonard Tuck, Vadim Glowna, Joe Hembus,
        Christopher Doherty, from ideas from a novel by
        Joseph Conrad.
Cam.:   Martin Schäfer.
Mus.:   Jürgen Knieper.
Prod.:  Atossa/ZDF.
Act.:   Jürgen Prochnow, Sam Waterston, Susanna
        Hamilton, Mario Adorf, Dominique Pinon.
94 min.

1990 *Das deutsche Kettensägenmassaker* (*The German Chain Saw Massacre*)

In a hotel, a butcher and his family chop up citizens of the former
German Democratic Republic with a chain saw; the idea serves as
an allegory for the problems encountered through German
Reunification.

Dir.:      Christoph Schlingensief.
SP.:       Christoph Schlingensief.
Cam.:      Christoph Schlingensief, Voxi Bärenklau.
Prod.:     DEM Film/Rhewes Filmproduktion.
Act.:      Karina Fallenstein, Susanne Bredehöft, Volker
           Spengler, Alfred Edel, Brigitte Kausch.
63 min.

1986  *Didi auf vollen Touren  (Didi Goes Wild)*

Comedy about a truck driver who is driving a load of used oil to a
dump in France. He unwittingly becomes involved in a cover-up for
an unscrupulous chemical company.

Dir.:      Wigbert   Wicker,   Robert   Menegoz   (action
           sequences).
SP.:       Felix Huby, Christoph Treutwein, Robert Menegoz,
           Dieter Hallervorden.
Cam.:      Josef Vilsmeier.
Mus.:      Uwe Borgward.
Prod.:     Ufa.
Act.:      Dieter Hallervorden, Bernard Menez, Hans-Peter
           Hallwachs, Pierre Tornade, Gert Haucke.
92 min.

1985  *Didi und die Rache der Enterbten (Didi Times Seven)*

A distant relative of the late Gustav Böllemann, unaware that he is
the wealthy banker's only heir, suddenly finds himself the target of
murder plots.

Dir.:      Christian Rateuke, Dieter Hallervorden.
SP.:       Christian Rateuke, Hartmann Schmige.
Cam.:      Günter Marczinkowsky.
Mus.:      Harold Faltermeier.
Prod.:     UFA-Filmproduktion.
Act.:      Dieter Hallervorden, Wolfgang Kieling, Gerhard
           Wollner, Margit Geissler.
92 min.

## 1986 (Turkish-Swiss-German) *Dilan*

Dilan, the beautiful daughter of a shepherd in East Anatolia, has two admirers. The one is poor but honest, the other wealthy. When Dilan's family chooses the poor man, the rich man's father steps in to ruin the wedding.

Dir.:    Erden Kiral.
SP.:    Omer Polat, Erden Kiral.
Cam.:    Martin Gressmann.
Mus.:    Nizymettin.
Prod.:    Hakan/Limbo/ZDF.
Act.:    Derya Arbas, Hakan Balamir, Ylmaz Zafer, Mahmet Erikci, Göler Okten.
90 min.

## 1987-88 *Doppelgänger (Double)*

A poor student gets an opportunity to live in a luxurious penthouse for a few days while its owner, a dead ringer for the student, is away. It turns out that the owner is a pathological secret agent, and the student is supposed to supply his alibi.

Dir.:    Emanuel Boeck.
SP.:    Wolf Christian Schroeder.
Cam.:    Karl Kases.
Mus.:    Jacques Zwart.
Prod.:    Late Show/Imperial/ Starlight.
Act.:    Uwe Ochsenknecht, Angie Hill, Michelle Evans, Simon Oates, Markus Dentler.
90 min.

## 1990 *Der doppelte Nötzli (Nötzli Twice)*

A clumsy chicken farmer from the Swiss provinces comes to Berlin to take care of the hotel belonging to his supposedly deceased twin brother, only to discover that the hotel is being used as a bordello.

Dir.:    Stefan Lukschy.

SP.:     Stefan Lukschy, Walter Roderer.
Cam.:    Peter Baumgartner.
Mus.:    Walter Baumgartner.
Prod.:   Ascot.
Act.:    Walter Roderer, Lolita Morena, Jeannine Burch,
         Ursula Heyer, Gunter Berger.
96 min.

## 1989 (German-French-Italian) *Dr. M*

The owner of a media empire uses a model and the electronic media
to drive people to commit suicide, because he needs their "energy" as
power backup for his steel heart.

Dir.:    Claude Chabrol.
SP.:     Sollange Mitchell, Thomas Bauermeister, Claude
         Chabrol, freely adapted from a novel by Norbert
         Jacques.
Cam.:    Jean Rabier.
Mus.:    Paul Hindemith, Mekong Delta.
Prod.:   NEF/ ZDF/Telefilm/La Sept/Ellepi/Clea.
Act.:    Alan Bates, Jennifer Beals, Jan Niklas, Hanns
         Zischler, Benoit Regent.
116 min.

## 1987 *Drachenfutter (Dragon's Food)*

A Pakistani refugee, who is seeking his fortune in Hamburg, and a
Chinese waiter attempt to realize their dreams of a better existence.
On the eve of the restaurant's opening, the Pakistani is deported.

Dir.:    Jan Schütte.
SP.:     Jan Schütte, Thomas Strittmayer.
Cam.:    Lutz Konermann.
Mus.:    Claus Bantzer.
Prod.:   Novoskop/Probst/ZDF.
Act.:    Bhasker, Ric Young, Buddy Uzzaman, Ulrich
         Wildgruber, Wolf-Dieter Sprenger.
79 min. (16mm)

1985 *Drei gegen drei - The Trio Film (Three against Three)*

Three German men are kidnapped to be exchanged for three nearly
identical South American generals. The latter can expect wealth, the
former death.

Dir.:     Dominik Graf.
SP.:      Martin Gies, Bernd Schwamm.
Cam.:     Klaus Eichhammer.
Mus.:     Andreas Köbner, Trio.
Prod.:    Neue Constantin.
Act.:     Stephan Remmler, Gert "Kralle" Krawinkel, Peter
          Behrens, Sunnyi Melles, Ralf Wolter, Peer
          Augustinski.
100 min.

1989 *Du Elvis - Ich Monroe (You Elvis - Me Monroe)*

A Turkish woman, who lives with her daughter in a Berlin apartment
house and is struggling to be self-sufficient, falls in love with an Arab
man who moves into the building.

Dir.:     Lothar Lambert.
SP.:      Lothar Lambert.
Cam.:     Lothar Lambert, Albert Kittler.
Prod.:    Lothar Lambert Prod.
Act.:     Baduri, Nilgün Taifun, Inga Schrader, Susanne
          Gautier, Erika Rabau.
70 min.

1986 *Du mich auch (And the Same to You)*

Two young people in present-day Berlin search for their first real
love, and end up in conflict with the underworld.

Dir.:     Anja Franke, Dani Levy, Helmut Berger.
SP.:      Anja Franke.
Cam.:     Carl-Friedrich Koschnick.
Mus.:     Nicki Reiser.

Prod.: Känguruh-Filmproduktion/Filmkollektiv Zürich.
Act.: Anja Franke, Dani Levy, Jens Naumann, Karleen Rutherford, Helma Fehrmann.
85 min.

1985 (German-Swiss) *Edvige Scimitt - Ein Leben zwischen Liebe und Wahnsinn* (*Edvige Scimitt - A Life between Love and Insanity*)

The life story of a young servant girl from the country at the turn of the century and her search for security.

Dir.: Matthias Zschokke.
SP.: Matthias Zschokke.
Cam.: Adrian Zschokke.
Mus.: Heiner Goebbels.
Prod.: Von Vietinghoff/ZDF/Xanadu.
Act.: Ingrid Kaiser, Fritz Schediwy, Wolfgang Michael, Klaus Volker, Miriam Spoerri.
90 min.

1988 *Der Einbruch The Accomplice*

A woman becomes the accomplice of a man who breaks into her home.

Dir.: Bettina Woernle.
SP.: Bettina Woernle.
Cam.: Werner Kubny.
Mus.: Manfred Schoof.
Prod.: Gerd Hecker.
Act.: Aurore Clement, Laurent Le Doyen, Ingrid van Bergen, Claus Dieter Reents, Jürgen Flimm.
103 min.

1990 *Das einfache Glück* (*A Little Happiness*)

Frank, a born loser from the wrong side of the tracks, has an argument with his lover while driving and hits a pedestrian, then flees the scene. Unfortunately, he confesses his deed to a small-time hood who then blackmails him.

Dir.:    Edzard Onneken.
SP.:     Edzard Onneken.
Cam.:    Bernhard Winkler.
Mus.:    Azra.
Prod.:   B.A./Skafander Prod.
Act.:    Jürgen Tonkel, Stefan Kuno, Adriane Pestalozzi,
         Anton Rattinger, Jockel Tschiersch.
95 min.

1985 *Die Einsteiger (The Gatecrashers)*

A video buff discovers how to "drop" into the plots of various video dramas, enabling himself and a friend to experience various genres of drama.

Dir.:    Siggi Götz.
SP.:     Mike Krüger, Thomas Gottschalk.
Cam.:    Heinz Hölscher.
Mus.:    Olaf Weitzl, Gerhard Heinz.
Prod.:   Lisa/K.S./Roxy.
Act.:    Mike Krüger, Thomas Gottschalk, Werner Kreindl,
         Kurt Weinzierl, Anja Kruse.
102 min.

1988 *Eis (Ice)*

A young man is unintentionally held in a jail cell for eighteen days with no food or water in his hometown in Austria.

Dir.:    Berthold Mittermayr.
SP.:     Berthold Mittermayr.
Cam.:    Ingo Hamer.
Mus.:    Georg Mittermayr.
Prod.:   Stefan Reiß Filmproduktion/BR.
Act.:    Erwin Leder, Michelle Sterr, Dagmar Cassens, Ulf
         Dieter Kusdas, Holde Naumann.
105 min.

1985 (German-Israeli) *Eis am Stiel 6. Teil - Ferienliebe (Lemon*

*Popsicle VI: Vacation Romance)*

Three teenage boys experience love and sex during a cruise.

> Dir.: Dan Wolman.
> SP.: Eli Davor, Sam Waynberg, Dan Wolman.
> Cam.: Ilan Rosenberg.
> Prod.: KF Kinofilm/Golan-Globus.
> Act.: Zachi Noy, Jesse Katzur, Petra Kogelnik, Bea Fiedler, Yehuda Afroni.
> 86 min.

1986 (German-Israeli) *Eis am Stiel, 7. Teil - Verliebte Jungs (Lemon Popsicle VII: Boys in Love)*

Three friends go on vacation together to search for sexual adventure, but one finds "real love."

> Dir.: Walter Bannert.
> SP.: Anton Moho.
> Cam.: Hanus Polak.
> Mus.: Hits of the 50s.
> Prod.: KF Kinofilm.
> Act.: Jesse Katzur, Zachi Noy, Jonathan Segal, Sonja Martin, Sissi Liebold.
> 91 min.

1988 (Israeli-German) *Eis am Stiel, 8. Teil - Summertime Blues (Lemon Popsicle VIII: West of Eden)*

Three young men want to open a disco on the beach, but they don't have enough money, so they have to be nice to the daughter of the man who is leasing them the building.

> Dir.: Reinhard Schwabenitzky.
> SP.: Reinhard Schwabenitzky.
> Cam.: Karl Kases.
> Mus.: Hits of the 60s.
> Prod.: KF Kinofilm.

Act.:    Zachi Noy, Jesse Katzur, Jonathan Segal, Elfi
         Eschke, Sibylle Rauch.
90 min.

1987 (German-Turkish) *Eisenerde - Kupferhimmel (Iron Earth -
Copper Sky)*

The citizens of a small Anatolian mountain village live in constant
fear of their greedy mayor, until they elect a "Saviour" who, through
many small "miracles," makes their lives more bearable.

Dir.:    Zülfü Livaneli.
SP.:     Zülfü Livaneli, from a novel by Yachar Kemal.
Cam.:    Jürgen Jürges.
Mus.:    Zülfü Livaneli.
Prod.:   Road-Movies/Interfilm/WDR.
Act.:    Rutkay Aziz, Yavuzer Cetinkaya, Macide Tanir,
         Gürel Yontan, Serap Aksoy.
98 min.

1989 *Elektro-Lähmung - Ein Film gegen die Ohnmacht (Electro-
Paralysis - A Movie Against Powerlessness)*

A group of people who are against the "Atomic Energy Mafia" call
upon fellow citizens to turn off all escalators, in order to fight against
what they call "electro-paralysis."

Dir.:    Bernward Wember.
SP.:     Bernward Wember.
Cam.:    Carlos Bustamente, Bernward Wember.
Prod.:   Bernward   Wember   Filmprod./Hamburger
         Filmbüro/ Hochschule der Künste, Berlin.
Act.:    Eva Mattes, Jörg Hube, Helma Fehrmann, Ingrid
         Ollrogge, Günther Jankowiak.
113 min.

1988 *Der entwendete Brief (The Purloined Letter)*

Edgar Allan Poe's story about the master detective, Auguste Dupin, and his efforts to regain possession of a letter that was stolen for the purpose of blackmail.

Dir.:    Stephan Bender.
SP.:     Stephan Bender.
Cam.:    Peter Esester, Frank-Guido Blasberg.
Mus.:    Rudolf Svatunek.
Prod.:   DFFB.
Act.:    Malgoscha Gebel, Paulus Manker, Gerard Krieger, Frank Behnke, Ostap Bender, Jr.
65 min.

1988 *Erdenschwer Earthbound*

The story of Franz Seeliger, who is locked away in an insane asylum and whose only dream is to overcome earth's gravity and soar through the air.

Dir.:    Oliver Herbrich.
SP.:     Oliver Herbrich, Andreas Hamburger, Friedemann Schultz (dialogues).
Cam.:    Ludolph Weyer.
Prod.:   Calypso/WDR.
Act.:    Johannes Thanheiser, Very Tschechowa, Rüdiger Vogler, Hark Bohm, Alfred Edel.
94 min.

1984 *Erst die Arbeit und dann? (First the Work, and Then What?)*

A short movie about a north German farm worker who puts in 14-hour days on the job, but who then goes on "R and R" through the "yuppie" bars of Hamburg.

Dir.:    Detlev Buck.
SP.:     Detlev Buck.
Cam.:    Burkhard Wellmann.
Mus.:    Detlev Brozat.
Prod.:   cult film-tv.
Act.:    Detlev Buck, Ella Nitzsche, Gerhard Ramm,

Chantalle Krüger.
43 min.

1989  (German-Soviet-French)  *Es ist nicht leicht ein Gott zu sein*
*(Hard to Be a God)*

In the thirtieth century, astronauts, who have long since overcome all
base instincts, search for a planet on which the people still possess
them.

Dir.:   Peter Fleischmann.
SP.:    Peter Fleischmann, Jean Claude Carriere, from a
        novel by Arkadij and Boris Strugatzki.
Cam.:   Pawel Lebeschew, Klaus-Müller Laue.
Mus.:   Jürgen Fritz.
Prod.:  Hallelujah   Film/ZDF/Studio   Dowschenko
        Kiew/Sofinfilm/Garance/Mediactuel/B.A./Media
        Actuell.
Act.:   Edward  Zentara,  Alexander  Filipenko,  Anne
        Gautier, Christine Kaufmann, Hugues Quester.
119 min.

1985  (German-Spanish)  *Escape to Paradise*

A businessman is supposed to bring young Melody to Tenerife, where
she is to work as an au pair, but instead, he flies her in his private jet
to the Bahamas, where she is to help free his son of the son's
Oedipus complex.

Dir.:   Hubert Frank.
SP.:    Hubert Frank.
Cam.:   Frank X. Lederle.
Mus.:   Gerhard Heinz.
Prod.:  Festival/Producciones Cinematograficas.
Act.:   Natalie  Moore,  Alfred  Bert,  Charles  Bexter,
        Victoria Vivas, Lila Ramon.
89 min.

1988 *Europa, abends  (Europe, at Dusk)*

A successful executive is assigned to arrange takeovers of other companies. At first, he enjoys the new challenge, but eventually comes to see his job as contributing to the destruction of Europe.

Dir.: Claudia Schröder.
SP.: Claudia Schröder.
Cam.: Igor Feldstein.
Prod.: Lichtblick/Igelfilm.
Act.: Christoph Moosbrugger, Maja Maranow, Heinz Schubert, Eddie Constantine, Susanne Beck.
85 min.

1987 *Der Experte  (Nonstop Troubles with The Experts)*

An auto mechanic has an accident and loses his memory. Due to a mix-up, he takes the place of an American election strategist and becomes an expert in campaign slogans for a fictitious West German political party.

Dir.: Reinhard Schwabenitzky.
SP.: Hartmann Schmige, Christian Rateuke.
Cam.: Josef Vilsmeier.
Mus.: Konstantin Wecker.
Prod.: Ufa.
Act.: Dieter Hallervorden, Klaus Guth, Steven Bennett, Walo Lüönd, Peter Fricke.
93 min.

1988  (German-Czech)  *Fabrik der Offiziere  (The Officer Factory)*

A lieutenant, who is the director of an officer's academy in the year
1944, solves the case of his predecessor's death, thus making some
powerful enemies.

Dir.:  Wolf Vollmar.
SP.:  Wolf Vollmar, from a novel by Hans Hellmut Kirst.
Cam.:  Ivan Slapeta.
Mus.:  Emil Viklicky.
Prod.:  Mondara-Film/Filmmove Studio Barrandov.
Act.:  Manfred Zapatka, Karl-Heinz Diess, Thomas
Holzmann, Harald Dietl, Stephan Meyer-Kohlhoff.
119 min.

1986  (German-Belgian)  *Der Fall Boran  (The Case of Boran)*

After being released from prison, a former gangster makes it big as
a movie star in criminal roles.  When his younger brother is shot
during a robbery, the ex-con must prove that he had nothing to do
with it.

Dir.:  Daniel Zuta.
SP.:  Daniel Zuta, Bernard Rud.
Cam.:  Walther van den Ende.
Mus.:  Okko Bekker, Jan Krueger, Lonzo Westphal.
Prod.:  Daniel Zuta Filmprod./Alain Keytsman Prod.
Act.:  Bernard Rud, Julien Schoenaerts, Renee Soutendijk,
Jean Pierre Leaud, Mia Griyp.
96 min.

1987  *Die Farbe der Indios  (The Colors of the Indios)*

A German boy, who lives in the big city with all the imaginable media available to him, dreams about an Indio boy of the same age who lives in the threatened rain forests of Brazil.

> Dir.:   Klaus Lautenbacher.
> SP.:    Klaus Lautenbacher.
> Cam.:   Klaus Lautenbacher.
> Prod.:  Antares.
> Act.:   Dotsche Ascopane, Klaus Lautenbacher, Leonore Paurat.
> 63 min. (16mm)

## 1987-88  *Faust*

The character of Faust here is a modern researcher who, in his fight for existential understanding, overlooks the ethical challenges of science and feels no responsibility towards life and ecology.

> Dir.:   Dieter Dorn.
> SP.:    Dieter Dorn, from the play by Johann Wolfgang von Goethe.
> Cam.:   Gernot Roll.
> Mus.:   Roger Jannotta.
> Prod.:  Bavaria/SDR.
> Act.:   Helmut Griem, Romuald Pekny, Sunnyi Melles, Cornelia Froboess, Rolf Boysen.
> 169 min.

## 1987  *Felix*

Felix's wife leaves him because he can't get along with women. He seeks comfort and love elsewhere, but eventually returns home, as does his wife. Story in four parts with four different female directors.

### 1.  *Er am Ende  (At Wit's End)*

> Dir.:   Helma Sanders-Brahms.
> SP.:    Helma Sanders-Brahms.
> Cam.:   Frank Brühne.

Act.:    Ulrich Tukur.

## 2. *Muß ich aufpassen (Do I Have to Be Careful?)*

Dir.:    Helke Sander.
SP.:     Helke Sander.
Cam.:    Martin Gressmann.
Act.:    Ulrich Tukur, Danuta Lato, Gabriele Herz.

## 3. *Eva*

Dir.:    Margarethe von Trotta.
SP.:     Margarethe von Trotta.
Cam.:    Franz Rath.
Act.:    Ulrich Tukur, Eva Matthes, Anette Uhlen.

## 4. *Are You Lonesome Tonight?*

Dir.:    Christel Buschmann.
SP.:     Christel Buschmann.
Cam.:    Mike Gast, Frank Brühne.
Act.:    Ulrich Tukur, Barbara Auer, August Zirner.
Prod.:   Futura.
86 min.

## 1990 *Feuer, Eis & Dynamit (Fire, Ice and Dynamite)*

A wealthy industrialist fakes his own death and prepares a strange will and testament in order to find out who is most deserving of inheriting his millions.

Dir.:    Willy Bogner.
SP.:     Tony Williamson.
Cam.:    Charly Steinberger.
Mus.:    Harold Faltermeyer.
Prod.:   Willy Bogner Film.
Act.:    Roger Moore, Shari Belafonte, Geoffrey Moore, Uwe Ochsenknecht.
106 min.

## 1985  *Feuer und Eis  (Fire and Ice)*

A young Swiss skier follows the woman he adores to New York and then to Aspen.

| | |
|---|---|
| Dir.: | Willy Bogner. |
| SP.: | Willy Bogner. |
| Cam.: | Willy Bogner. |
| Mus.: | Harold Faltermeyer, Gary Wright, Allan Parsons Project, Panarama. |
| Prod.: | Willy Bogner Film. |
| Act.: | John Eaves, Suzy Chaffee, Tom Slims, Steve Link, Kelby Anno. |

90 min.

## 1988  *Fifty-Fifty*

A young man from a wealthy family decides to rob a bank to get his family to notice him. He ends up taking two hostages who eventually demand to share the "take" with him.

| | |
|---|---|
| Dir.: | Peter Timm. |
| SP.: | Detlef Michel. |
| Cam.: | Fritz Seemann. |
| Mus.: | City. |
| Prod.: | Aspekt-Telefilm/Ottokar Runze/ZDF. |
| Act.: | Heinz Hoenig, Dominique Horwitz, Suzanne von Borsody, Siegfried Kernen, Karl Friedrich. |

90 min.

## 1986  *Der Flieger  (The Glider)*

The story of a young man whose fascination with hanggliding gets his whole provincial town into an uproar.

| | |
|---|---|
| Dir.: | Erwin Keusch. |
| SP.: | Uwe Timm. |
| Cam.: | Jürgen Jürges. |
| Mus.: | Andreas Köbner. |

Prod.: Xenofilm/prokino/ZDF.
Act.: Martin May, Ulrike Kriener, Birgit Franz, Norbert Mahler, Dieter Augustin.
107 min.

1987 (German-Austrian) *Der Fluch (The Curse)*

A family outing in the mountains ends in horror when the family discovers that they have been cursed.

Dir.: Ralf Huettner.
SP.: Andy T. Hoetzel, Ralf Huettner.
Cam.: Diethard Prengel.
Mus.: Andreas Köbner.
Prod.: Extrafilm/BR/SDR/ORF.
Act.: Dominic Raacke, Barbara May, Romina Nowack, Ortrud Beginnen, Gero Lohmeyer.
92 min.

1985-86 (German-Finnish) *Flucht in den Norden (Escape to the North)*

From the novel by Klaus Mann, which tells the story of a young German communist living in exile in Finland in 1933 who is faced with the dilemma of remaining true to his ideals or having a happy life in his own country.

Dir.: Ingemo Engström.
SP.: Ingemo Engström, from a novel by Klaus Mann.
Cam.: Axel Block.
Mus.: Johann S. Bach, Jean Sibelius.
Prod.: Theuring-Engström/Jörn Donner Prod.
Act.: Katharina Thalbach, Jukka-Pekka Palo, Lena Olin, Käbi Lareti, Tom Poysti.
126 min.

1982 *Die Flügel der Nacht (The Wings of the Night)*

An employee of the "Cultural Institute for Social Integration," which is supposed to further the general harmonization of society, disappears one day and flees to Finland, where he falls in love and attempts to start a new life.

Dir.: Hans Noever.
SP.: Hans Noever, Ursula Jeshel.
Cam.: Robert Alazraki.
Prod.: DNS-Film/Popular Film/BR.
Act.: Michael König, Christine Boisson, Armin Mueller-Stahl, Laurens Straub, Reinhard Firchow.
88 min.

1985 *Die Föhnforscher (Föhn Researchers)*

A partly political film with provocative social criticism of the Federal Republic.

Dir/SP.: Herbert Achternbusch.
Cam.: Adam Olech, Stefano Guidi.
Prod.: Herbert Achternbusch.
Act.: Gabi Geist, Herbert Achternbusch, Franz Baumgartner, Hartmut Geerken, Sigrid Geerken.
132 min.

1988 *Follow Me*

This film uses the example of a philosophy professor in modern-day Prague who is forced to work as an airport porter to show the fate of those who criticized the government in communist Czechoslovakia.

Dir.: Maria Knilli.
SP.: Maria Knilli, Vera Has.
Cam.: Klaus Eichhammer, Reiner Lauter.
Mus.: Tzvetan Marangosoff.
Prod.: Alpha-Film/Allianz-Film.
Act.: Pavel Landovsky, Marina Vlady, Katharina Thalbach, Rudolf Wessely, Ulrich Reinthaller.
102 min.

1985  *Der Formel Eins Film (Feel the Motion)*

A young woman tries to get on a television musical show.

Dir.:  Wolf Büld.
SP.:  Wolf Büld, Rochus Hahn, Peter Zemann.
Cam.:  Roland Willaert.
Mus.:  Various hit songs.
Prod.:  Solaris Film/Bavaria/Neue Constantin.
Act.:  Sissy Kelling, Frank Meyer-Brockmann, Ingolf Lück,
      Tote Hosen, Pia Zadora.
101 min.

1986  *Francesca*

The fictional biography of a woman who grew up as an orphan in a
Bavarian convent and became a famous musician, dancer and actress
in Italy.

Dir.:  Verena Rudolph.
SP.:  Verena Rudolph.
Cam.:  Eberhard Gieck.
Mus.:  Fulvio Di Stefano, Leopoldo Sanfelice.
Prod.:  Heide Breitel Filmprod./Verena Rudolph/ZDF.
Act.:  Eva Lissa, Dorothea Neff, Bernhard Wosien, Dolly
      Würzbach, Olga von Togni.
95 min.

1988  (Italian-German)  *Franziskus*

Following the death of St. Francis of Assisi in 1226, his followers
gather and tell the story of his life and deeds.

Dir.:  Liliana Cavani.
SP.:  Liliana Cavani, Roberta Mazzoni, taken from a
      historical novel by Hermann Hesse.
Cam.:  Giuseppe Lanci, Ennio Guranieri.
Mus.:  Vangelis.
Prod.:  Karol/Radio  Italia  Uno/Italmoleggio

Cinematografico/Royal.
Act.: Mickey Rourke, Helena Bonham Carter, Fabio Bussotti, Hanns Zischler, Paolo Bonacelli.
124 min.

1986 (French-German) *Die Frau meines Lebens* *(The Woman of my Dreams)*

A violin soloist develops a drinking problem, which nearly ruins his marriage and drives away his friends.

Dir.: Regis Wargnier.
SP.: Regis Wargnier.
Cam.: Francis Catonne.
Mus.: Romano Musumarra.
Prod.: Odessa/TF1/Bioskop/HR.
Act.: Christophe Malvoy, Jane Birkin, Jean-Louis Trintignant, Beatrice Agenin, Andrzej Seweryn.
102 min.

1990 *Eine Frau namens Harry* *(Harry and Harriet)*

A young woman who lives in a society dominated by men makes a pact with the devil so that she can change her gender and see what it is like to have the professional and financial advantages that men enjoy.

Dir.: Cyril Frankel.
Cam.: Heinz Hölscher.
Prod.: Lisa/K.S. Film/Roxy/Monaco.
Act.: Thomas Gottschalk, Fiona Fullerton, Heinz Hoenig, Mandy Perryment, Heinz Mareck.
95 min.

1989 *Fünf Bier und ein Kaffee* *(Five Beers and a Coffee)*

Five young people in Berlin wile away their time drinking and making music, until one of them ends up in a psychiatric clinic, where he makes the acquaintance of a singer from the 30s who helps him escape.

Dir.: Rudolf Steiner.
SP.: Sami Kovacevic, Bernd Manzke, Volker Guhlich, Rudolf Steiner.
Cam.: Volker Tittel.
Mus.: Alexander Kraut, Gustl Lüdjes.
Prod.: Rudolf Steiner Filmproduktion/ZDF.
Act.: Sami Kovacevic, Michael Wrzesinski, Volker Guhlich, Bernd Manzke, Norman Herbst.
96 min.

1989 (German-English) *Der fünfte Freitag (Melancholia)*

A German art critic, living in London, experiences a major crisis in his life, then gets asked to murder a Chilean military doctor and known torturer.

Dir.: Andi Engel.
SP.: Andi Engel, Lewis Rodia.
Cam.: Denis Crossan.
Mus.: Simon Fisher Turner.
Prod.: Lichtblick/NDR/Filmfonds Hamburg/Hamburger Filmbüro/British Film Institute/Channel Four.
Act.: Jeroen Krabbe, Susannah York, Ulrich Wildgruber, Jane Gurnett, Kate Hardie.
87 min.

1986 (German-U.S.) *für immer: Lulu (Forever, Lulu)*

A young emigrant and would-be writer in New York has a string of bad luck and a series of adventures that bring her fame and fortune.

Dir.: Amos Kollek.
SP.: Amos Kollek.
Cam.: Lisa Rinzler.
Mus.: Paul Chiara Laszlo.
Prod.: Lulu Company/Dieter Geißler Filmprod./TV

60/TV-80 California/BR.
Act.:    Hanna Schygulla, Debbie Harry, Annie Golden,
         Alec Baldwin, Ruth Westheimer.
82 min.

1988 (Italian-German-French) *Fürchten und lieben (Love and Fear)*

Three sisters attempt to overcome personal and ideological
difficulties, even though their male counterparts in their family are
incapable of joining in this struggle.

Dir.:    Margarethe von Trotta.
SP.:     Margarethe von Trotta, Dacia Maraini, patterned
         after a play by Anton Chekhov.
Cam.:    Giuseppe Lanci.
Mus.:    Franco Piersanti.
Prod.:   Erre Produzioni/Bioskop/Cinemax-Generale
         d'Image.
Act.:    Fanny Ardant, Greta Scacchi, Valeria Golino, Peter
         Simonischek, Jan Biczycki.
112 min.

1986 (Czech-German-Austrian) *Galöschen des Glücks (Lucky Galoshes)*

Two fairies who help people by means of magic galoshes cause a great deal of confusion in 19th-century Copenhagen.

Dir.: Juraj Herz.
SP.: Alex Königsmark, Juraj Herz, from a fairy tale by Hans Christian Andersen.
Cam.: Jozef Simoncic.
Mus.: Michael Kocab, Carl Maria von Weber, Josef Strauss.
Prod.: Koliba Studio Bratislava/Slovensky Film/Omnia/MR-Film/ZDF/ORF.
Act.: Jana Brejchova, Towje Kleiner, Luis Lopez Vasquez, Miroslav Donutil, Jan Hrusinsky Jr.
90 min.

1985 (German-French) *Gefahr für die Liebe - AIDS (Perils of Love-AIDS)*

A drug addict manages to get clean and now earns a good living as a taxi driver. Everything is going well for him and his girlfriend, when he discovers he has AIDS.

Dir.: Hans Noever.
SP.: Paul Hengge.
Cam.: Hans-Günther Bücking.
Mus.: Francis Lai, Roland Romanelli.
Prod.: CCC Filmkunst/DGF/KG/Lira-Films.
Act.: Fritz Cat, Geraldine Danon, Piero von Arnim, Oliver Rohrbeck, Oliver Pascalin.
88 min.

53

1987  *Die Geierwally  (Geierwally)*

Movie version of the novel by Wilhelmine von Hillern about young
Geierwally who is told by her father to marry a man she doesn't love,
even though she really does love another.

Dir.:     Walter Bockmayer.
SP.:      Walter Bockmayer, from a novel by Wilhelmine von
          Hillern.
Cam.:     Wolfgang Simon.
Mus.:     Horst Hornung.
Prod.:    Entenfilm/Pro-ject/ZDF.
Act.:     Samy Orfgen, Gottfried Lackmann, Christoph
          Eichhorn, Elisabeth Volkmann, Ralf Morgenstern.
91 min.

1988  *Gekauftes Glück  (Bride of the Orient)*

A Swiss farmer sends for a Thai bride in order to be able to run his
farm more efficiently.   While his relationship with his new wife
improves steadily, he has to deal with gossip and jealousy from the
other villagers.

Dir.:     Urs Odermatt.
SP.:      Urs Odermatt.
Cam.:     Rainer Klausmann.
Mus.:     Frederic Chopin, Franz Schubert, etc.
Prod.:    Balance Film/Cinefilm.
Act.:     Wolfram Berger, Arunotai Jitreekan, Werner
          Herzog, Mathias Gnädinger, Günter Meisner.
98 min.

1988-89  *Geld  (Money)*

With an unemployed husband and bill collectors knocking at her
door, a woman decides to rob her bank and take its manager (her
neighbor) as hostage. Comedy.

Dir.:     Doris Dörrie.

SP.:     Doris Dörrie, Michael Juncker.
Cam.:    Helge Weindler.
Mus.:    Philip Johnston.
Prod.:   Olga-Film/ZDF.
Act.:    Billie Zöckler, Uwe Ochsenknecht, Sunnyi Melles,
         August Zirner, Ulrike Kriener.
98 min.

1986  *Geld oder Leber  (Your Money or your Liver)*

A couple of small-time hoods succeed in acquiring a large number of
gems, but hide them inside of a deep-frozen goose, which gets sold.

Dir.:    Dieter Pröttel.
SP.:     Christoph Treutwein, Mike Krüger.
Cam.:    Atze Glanert.
Mus.:    Gerhard Heinz, Erste Allgemeine Verunsicherung,
         Falco.
Prod.:   Lisa/K.S./Roxy.
Act.:    Mike Krüger, Ursela Monn, Falco, Raimund
         Harmstorf, Barbara Valentin.
85 min.

1989  *Georg Elser - Einer aus Deutschland  (Georg Elser, One Man
from Germany)*

The story of the Swabian clockmaker, Johann Georg Elser, who, on
November 8, 1939, attempted to assassinate Adolf Hitler in a beer
hall in Munich with a homemade bomb.

Dir.:    Klaus Maria Brandauer.
SP.:     Stephen Shepard, from his novel.
Cam.:    Kajos Koltai.
Mus.:    Georges Delerue.
Prod.:   Söhnlein/Borman    Produktion/Mutoskop    Film
         Saturn Movie.
Act.:    Klaus Maria Brandauer, Brian Dennehy, Rebecca
         Miller, Elisabeth Orth, Nigel Le Vaillant.
97 min.

1985 *German Dreams*

After being imprisoned for eighteen months for trying to escape the German Democratic Republic, a woman and her sixteen-year-old daughter are deported by the government to West Berlin. This new "Golden West" does not turn out to be the haven she was hoping for.

Dir.: Lienhard Wawrzyn.
SP.: Lienhard Wawrzyn.
Cam.: Claus Deubel.
Mus.: Jürgen Buchner.
Prod.: Regina Ziegler/WDR/DFFB.
Act.: Angela Leiberg, Ilona Lewanowski, Hans-Henning Borgelt, Hans Lerman, Ilja Schellschmidt.
88 min.

1989 (German-American) *Die Geschichte der Dienerin* *(The Handmaid's Tale)*

Movie version of Margaret Atwood's best-selling novel, which portrays a future society ruled by religious fundamentalists where women are valued only for their reproductive abilities.

Dir.: Volker Schlöndorff.
SP.: Harold Pinter, from the novel by Margaret Atwood.
Cam.: Igor Luther.
Mus.: Ryuichi Sakamoto.
Prod.: Bioskop/CinecomInternational/Odyssey/Cinetudes Films.
Act.: Natasha Richardson, Faye Dunaway, Robert Duvall, Aidan Quinn, Elizabeth McGovern.
109 min.

1989 (German-USA) *Der Geschichtenerzähler* *(The Story Teller)*

The relationship between an ambitious young writer and his wealthy wife is strained to the breaking point.

Dir.: Rainer Boldt.

SP.:   Rainer Boldt, Dorothea Neukirchen, Wolf Christian Schröder.
Cam.:   Rold Liccini.
Mus.:   Serge Weber.
Prod.:   Helmut Wietz, Wilber Stark.
Act.:   Udo Schenk, Anke Sevenich, Christine Kaufmann, Peter Sattmann, Rüdiger Wandel.
95 min.

1987 (German-Austrian) *Gewitter im Mai (May Storms)*

At the turn of the century, a seaman returns to his Bavarian village, where he wins the love of his youth, even though she is then killed along with his rival for her affections.

Dir.:   Xaver Schwarzenberger.
SP.:   Jörg Graser, from a story by Ludwig Ganghofer.
Cam.:   Xaver Schwarzenberger.
Prod.:   Iduna/MR/ZDF/ORF.
Act.:   Gabriel Barylli, Claudia Messner, Michael Greiling, Michael Robin, Maria Emo.
94 min.

1985 (German-Italian-French) *Ginger und Fred (Ginger and Fred)*

Two aging dancers, who haven't seen each other for thirty years, meet up again at a special TV Christmas broadcast in Italy and recreate their imitation of Ginger Rogers and Fred Astaire.

Dir.:   Federico Fellini.
SP.:   Federico Fellini, Tonino Guerra, Tullio Pinelli.
Cam.:   Tonino Delli Colli, Ennio Guarnieri.
Mus.:   Nicola Piovani.
Prod.:   Stella/Bibo TV/Anthea/PEA/Revcom.
Act.:   Giulietta Masina, Marcello Mastroianni, Franco Fabrizi, Friedrich von Ledebur, Augusto Poderosi.

126 min.

1989 *Der Glanz dieser Tage* (*The Splendor of These Days*)

A married man is "called" to become a priest.

Dir.: Wenzel Storch.
SP.: Wenzel Storch.
Cam.: Wenzel Storch.
Mus.: Schweine im Weltall, Die Fliegenden Unterhosen, Hermann Naujoks und die Naujoks, Diet, etc.
Prod.: Wenzel Storch.
Act.: Jürgen Höhne, Alexandra Schwartz, Bernward Herkenrath, Sabine Meyer, Wenzel Storch.
93 min.

1987 *Der gläserne Himmel* (*The Glass Sky*)

In a dream, an office witnesses the murder of a mysterious woman in black. He follows her through Paris, where he finds himself in a secret world between dream and reality.

Dir.: Nina Grosse.
SP.: Nina Grosse, from a story by Julio Cortazar.
Cam.: Hans-Günther Bücking.
Mus.: Flora St. Loup.
Prod.: Avista Film/Voissfilm/Nina Grosse/BR.
Act.: Helmut Berger, Sylvie Orcier, Agnes Film, Maria Hartmann, Tobias Engel.
87 min.

1988 (German-Swiss) *Die Gottesanbeterin* (*Georgette*)

The young wife of a pharmacist is really in love with her own brother, but since she cannot have a satisfactory relationship with him, she begins murdering her lovers with poisoned kisses.

Dir.: Tania Stöckling, Cyrille Rey-Coquais.
SP.: Tania Stöckling, Cyrille Rey-Coquais, Felix Schneider-Henninger.
Cam.: Ciro Cappellari, Anka Schmid.

Mus.: Nikolaus Utermöhlen.
Prod.: DFFB/Stanley-Thomas-Johnson Stiftung.
Act.: Tiziana Jelmini, Thomas Schunke, Dina Leipzig, Kio Cornel Hedl, Detlev Knops.
82 min.

1986 (Italian-German) *Grüne Hölle von Cartagena (The Green Hell of Cartagena)*

An actress fights for her inheritance from her father in Colombia, aided by her half brother and a sailor, who later falls in love with her.

Dir.: Tommaso Dazzi.
SP.: Sergio Donati, Sauro Scavalino.
Cam.: Luigi Verda.
Mus.: Tony Esposito.
Prod.: Effe P.C. Produzioni Cine TV/SDR.
Act.: Franco Nero, Barbara de Rossi, Robert Barr, Franco Javaronne, Francisco Rabal.
87 min.

1989 *Gummibärchen küßt man nicht (Real Men Don't Eat Gummy Bears)*

A nineteen-year-old dropout searches for his father, who ran off before the boy's birth to seek his fortune in Africa.

Dir.: Walter Bannert.
SP.: Florian Burg.
Cam.: Hanus Polack.
Prod.: K.S. Film/Lisa.
Act.: Chris Mitchum, Robby Rosa, Bentley Mitchum, Angela Alvarado, Ernest Borgnine.
89 min.

1980 *Ein Guru kommt (A Guru is Coming)*

A down-and-out singer becomes the leader of an Indian religious commune, but is unable to hold on to his empire.

Dir.:    Rainer Erler.
SP.:     Rainer Erler.
Cam.:    Wolfgang Grasshoff.
Mus.:    Eugen Thomass.
Prod.:   pentagramma/ZDF.
Act.:    Wolfgang Reichmann,  Eric P. Caspar, Jörg Pleva,
         Wolfgang Kieling, Wolf Harnisch.
98 min.

## 1988  Hab ich nur Deine Liebe  (If I Only Have Your Love)

A young, successful computer expert in Hamburg has a less successful private life, until he meets a woman who can no longer talk, but expresses herself through song.

Dir.:    Peter Kern.
SP.:    Peter Kern.
Cam.:    Eberhard Geick.
Prod.:    Elisabeth Müller Filmprod./NDR.
Act.:    Christa Berndl, Tilo Prückner, Ankie Beilke-Lau, Marcelo Uriona, Brigitte Janner.
97 min.

## 1990  Die Hallo-Sisters  (The Hello Sisters)

A female singing duo who had great success in the 50s attempts a comeback.

Dir.:    Ottokar Runze.
SP.:    Richard Hey, Lisa Kristwaldt.
Cam.:    Michael Epp.
Prod.:    Ottokar Runze Filmprod./ ZDF.
Act.:    Gisela May, Else Werner, Harald Juhnke, Tuncel Kurtiz, Pit Krüger.
90 min.

## 1988  (German-Hungarian-Austrian)  Hanussen

Story of the life and fate of the variety show illusionist, Klaus Schneider, who in the 20s and 30s became famous as the great clairvoyant Eric Jan Hanussen.

Dir.:     Istvan Szabo.
SP.:     Istvan Szabo, Peter Dobai.
Cam.:     Lajos Koltai.
Prod.:     CCC/ZDF/Mafilm   Objektiv   Studio/Mokep/ Hungaro-Film/ORF.
Act.:     Klaus Maria Brandauer, Erland Josephson, Grazyna Szapolowska, Adriana Biedrzynska, Karoly Eperjes.
118 min.

1976   (Italian-German)   *Happy Birthday, Harry*

A womanizer and editor of a sex magazine must suddenly find a woman to marry him within two days, or forfeit his large inheritance.

Dir.:     Marius Mattei.
SP.:     Marius Mattei, Christian Lutz Laske.
Cam.:     Marcello Masciocchi, Angelo Fani.
Mus.:     German Weiss.
Prod.:     Pal International Films/H.L.U.F.S.
Act.:     John Richardson, Carola Andre, Marisa Mell, Terry Thomas, Eleonora Fani.
79 min.

1983   *Happy Weekend*

Film about a group of youths battling with a prudish mayor to allow a discotheque in their town.

Dir.:     Murray Jordan.
SP.:     Donald Arthur.
Cam.:     N/A.
Mus.:     Sam Spence.
Prod.:     Ufa/Scala (Video).
Act.:     Alfons Haider, Ingrid Richter, Petra Drechsler, Herbert Fux, Erich Fötzinger.
82 min.

1989   *Hard Days - Hard Nights*

Four inexperienced young musicians from Liverpool get a gig in Hamburg's red-light district in 1960. In spite of their success, they eventually fall apart due to drugs, orgies and prostitution.

Dir.: Horst Königstein.
SP.: Horst Königstein.
Cam.: Klaus Brix.
Mus.: Hans P. Ströer.
Prod.: Provobis/Projekt/NDR.
Act.: Rita Tushingham, Al Corley, Wigald Boning, Annette Hörmann, Tony Forsyth.
103 min.

## 1986 *Hatschipuh*

Children's movie about small, invisible imps who help a family in a Bavarian village who are being swindled out of their farm.

Dir.: Ulrich König.
SP.: Ulrich König, Franz Marischka.
Cam.: Franz Rath.
Mus.: Fritz Muschler, Joe Kleindienst.
Prod.: Checkpoint/Mutoskop/M & P/Robert van Ackeren Maran/SDR.
Act.: Toni Berger, Adelheid Arndt, Henry van Lyck, Michael Schwarzmaier, Jan Steinbeck.
95 min.

## 1985 (German-Austrian) *Heidenlöcher (Heidenlöcher)*

Winter 1942-43 in an Austrian mining village: A young man, disappointed at not being sent to the front, betrays a deserter, whom the villagers had been hiding, to the Gestapo.

Dir.: Wolfram Paulus.
SP.: Wolfram Paulus.
Cam.: Wolfgang Simon.
Mus.: Bert Breit.
Prod.: Voissfilm/Marwo/BR.

Act.:    Florian Pirchner, Albert Paulus, Helmut Vogel,
         Gerta Rettenwender, Rolf Zacher.
98 min.

1985  *Heilt Hitler!*  (*Heal Hitler!*)

After more than 40 years as a prisoner of war, Herbert makes it back
to Munich, which appears to him now to be a new Stalingrad.

Dir.:    Herbert Achternbusch.
SP.:     Herbert Achternbusch.
Cam.:    Herbert Schzild, Gunter Freyse, Adam Olech.
Prod.:   Herbert Achternbusch.
Act.:    Gunter Freyse, Herbert Achternbusch, Gabi Geist,
         Waltraud Galler, Annamirl Bierbichler.
140 min.

1987  (German-Finnish)  *Helsinki Napoli - All Night Long*

A Finnish taxi driver in Berlin discovers two dead bodies in his taxi,
but when he decides to "relieve" them of their money, he becomes the
target of a manhunt conducted by three American gangsters.

Dir.:    Mika Kaurismäki.
SP.:     Richard Reitinger, Mika Kaurismäki.
Cam.:    Helge Weindler.
Mus.:    Jacques Zwart.
Prod.:   Salinas/Villealfa.
Act.:    Kari Väänänen, Robert Manfredi, Jean-Pierre
         Castaldi, Margi Clarke, Nino Manfredi.
96 min.

1988  *Herbstmilch*  (*Autumn Milk*)

The story of a young woman in Bavaria in the years from 1938 to
1945. Her mother dies, leaving her to care for her large family and
farm. She marries, but her husband is drafted, and she must care for
his family as well.

Dir.:     Joseph Vilsmaier.
SP.:      Peter Steinbach, from the autobiography of Anna
          Wimschneider.
Cam.:     Joseph Vilsmaier.
Mus.:     Norbert Jürgen Schneider.
Prod.:    Perathon/ZDF.
Act.:     Dana Vavrova, Werner Stocker, Claude Oliver
          Rudolph, Eva Mattes, Ilona Mayer.
111 min.

1986-87 *Herz mit Löffel* (*Heart with a Spoon*)

A young retiree puts a personal ad in the paper, but adds as a
condition that the woman must cook a meal for him. Soon he has so
many invitations to dinner he doesn't know what to do!

Dir.:     Richard Blank.
SP.:      Otto Grünmandl, Richard Blank.
Cam.:     Vlada Majic.
Prod.:    Arno Film/B. A. Film/Project/Bioskop/Filmpool/
          BR.
Act.:     Otto Grünmandl, Rosel Zech, Hannelore Schroth,
          Adelheid Arndt.
85 min.

1990 *Herzlich willkommen* (*Hello and Welcome*)

After having been imprisoned for ten years, a twenty-six-year-old
flees the German Democratic Republic for the West. He gets a
training position working for an ex-Nazi in a reform school, befriends
a young orphan boy, and falls in love with one of the group leaders.

Dir.:     Hark Bohm.
SP.:      Hark Bohm, Dorothee Schön, from ideas from a
          novel by Walter Kempowski.
Cam.:     Edward Klosinski.
Mus.:     Jens Peter Ostendorf.
Prod.:    Hamburger Kinokompanie/ZDF.
Act.:     Uwe Bohm, David Bohm, Hark Bohm, Barbara

Auer, Michael Gwisdek.
92 min.

## 1990  *Hick's Last Stand*

The narrated travel diary of a man who is searching for myths and legends--and himself--in America.

Dir.:    Herbert Achternbusch.
SP.:    Herbert Achternbusch.
Cam.:  Cordula Smolka.
Prod.:  Herbert Achternbusch Filmprod.
Act.:    Herbert Achternbusch.
79 min.

## 1989  *High Score*

A man who is obsessed with video games accidentally kills someone and then flees the scene. The crime is investigated by a policeman who is no less obsessed with his electronic surveillance equipment.

Dir.:    Gustav Ehmck.
SP.:    Gustav Ehmck, Peter Lawrence.
Cam.:  Gerard Vandenberg.
Mus.:  Matthias Thurow.
Prod.:  Roxy/Ehmck/Filmtheaterbetriebe Pollit/BR.
Act.:    James Brolin, Gudrun Landgrebe, Jace Alexander, Anne Carlisle, Hannes Jaenicke.
93 min.

## 1986-87  (German-French)  *Der Himmel über Berlin  (Wings of Desire)*

An angel falls in love with a trapeze artist and comes to Earth as a mortal to become more familiar with the world and its people, especially those in the city of Berlin.

Dir.:    Wim Wenders.
SP.:    Wim Wenders, in cooperation with Peter Handke.

Cam.: Henri Alekan.
Mus.: Jürgen Knieper.
Prod.: Road Movie/Argos/WDR.
Act.: Bruno Ganz, Solveig Dommartin, Otto Sander, Curt Bois, Peter Falk.
127 min.

## 1988 *Himmelsheim*

The villagers in a small town are shocked when the federal train system brings dirt, noise and rumors that the village will be cut in two by the new train route.

Dir.: Manfred Stelzer.
SP.: Fitzgerald Kusz.
Cam.: Frans Bromet.
Mus.: Rio Reiser.
Prod.: Journal Film/Maran.
Act.: Elke Sommer, Siegfried Zimmerscheid, Gustl Augustin, Hanns Zischler, Anette Faverey.
89 min.

## 1987 *Hollywood Monster*

A young film director and his leading man search for a missing inheritance.

Dir.: Roland Emmerich.
SP.: Roland Emmerich, Thomas Kubisch.
Cam.: Karl Walter Lindenlaub.
Mus.: Hubert Bartholomae.
Prod.: Centropolis/Pro-ject/HR.
Act.: Jason Lively, Jill Whitlow, Tim McDaniel, Paul Gleason, Leonard Lansink.
112 min.

## 1989 *Hopnick*

Stories from the everyday life of a West Berlin customs official at a closed border crossing, whose job bores him to tears.

Dir.:    Detlev Buck.
SP.:     Roger Heereman, Detlev Buck, Hans E. Viet.
Cam.:    Roger Heereman.
Mus.:    Burkhard Brozat.
Prod.:   Deutsche Film- und Fernsehakademie Berlin.
Act.:    Detlev Buck, Hans E. Viet, Pago Balke, Sophie
         Rois, Andreas Hosang.
60 min.

1989  *Hundert Jahre Adolf Hitler - Die letzte Stunde im Führerbunker
(One Hundred Years of Adolf Hitler - The Last Hours in the Führer's
Bunker)*

An experimental film shot in a bunker from World War II. It tells
the story of Hitler's last hours.

Dir.:    Christoph Schlingensief.
SP.:     Christoph Schlingensief, from his play.
Cam.:    Foxi Bärenklau.
Mus.:    Tom Dokoupil.
Prod.:   DEM/Hymen II/Madeleine Remy.
Act.:    Volker  Spengler,  Brigitte  Kausch,  Margit
         Carstensen, Dietrich Kuhlbrodt, Alfred Edel.
60 min.

1989 (French-German) *Ich bin dir verfallen* *(I'm Your Slave)*

Story of a woman who has been a nun, a worker, a priest's lover and a trade union functionary, and the disillusionment she came to feel in each role.

Dir.: Jean-Pierre Thorn.
SP.: Jean-Pierre Thorn, Lorette Cordie, Dominique Lancelot.
Cam.: Denis Gheerbrant.
Mus.: Jacky Moreau.
Prod.: Les Films d'Ici/Video 13/La Sept/Road Movies.
Act.: Solveig Dommartin, Philippe Clevenot, Henri Serre, Aurore Prieto, Helene Surgere.
118 min.

1959 (German-Argentine) *Ich möchte mit dir leben* *(I Want to Live with You)*

The close friendship between a German orphan and an Argentinian boy is put to the test but prevails.

Dir.: Carlos Rinaldi.
SP.: Ramon Gomez Maria.
Mus.: Ribeo.
Prod.: Transocean-Film/Vasgen Badal & co./ International Films.
Act.: Alberto de Mendoza, Susanne Cramer, Guillermo Battaglia.
90 min.

1987 *Ich und Er (He and I)*

A young New Yorker wants to make it up the career ladder as an architect, but he faces difficulties when his genital organ begins acting--and talking--on its own.

| | |
|---|---|
| Dir.: | Doris Dörrie. |
| SP.: | Warren D. Leight, from a story by Alberto Moravia. |
| Cam.: | Helge Weindler. |
| Mus.: | Klaus Doldinger. |
| Prod.: | Neue Constantin. |
| Act.: | Griffin Dunne, Ellen Greene, Craig T. Nelson, Kelly Bishop, Carey Lowell. |
| 83 min. | |

1984-85 *Im Himmel ist die Hölle los* (*All Hell's Breaking Loose in Heaven*)

A TV star makes a guest appearance in a small town and causes an uproar with all his female fans there. One young woman manages to get a part in his show and wins his heart.

| | |
|---|---|
| Dir.: | Helmer von Lützelburg. |
| SP.: | Helmer von Lützelburg, Markus Klug. |
| Cam.: | Klaus Eichhammer, Horst Knechtel. |
| Mus.: | Markus Klug. |
| Prod.: | Emotion Pictures. |
| Act.: | Dirk Bach, Billie Zöckler, Barbara Valentin, Cleo Kretschmer, Walter Bockmeyer. |
| 82 min. | |

1987 *Im Jahr der Schildkröte* (*In the Year of the Turtle*)

A lonely 60-year-old man meets a "flipped-out" 20-year-old woman; after much skepticism and mistrust, they develop a warm and positive relationship.

| | |
|---|---|
| Dir.: | Ute Wieland. |
| SP.: | Ute Wieland, from a novel by Hans Werner Kettenbach. |
| Cam.: | Karl-Walter Lindenlaub. |

Mus.: Nick Glowna.
Prod.: Geissendörfer Film & Fernsehprod./WDR.
Act.: Heinz Bennent, Karina Fallenstein, Anke Tegtmeyer, Arpad Kraupa.
97 min.

1988 (German-Hungarian) *Im Süden meiner Seele (In The South of My Soul)*

A biographical film based on the life of Paul Celan.

Dir.: Frieder Schuller.
SP.: Frieder Schuller.
Cam.: K. Mihailescu, Vlad Paunescu.
Mus.: Cornel Taranu.
Prod.: Martin Häussler.
Act.: Gudrun Landgrebe, Michael Goldberg, Ion Besoiu, Csaba Körösi, Emilia Dobrin.
97 min.

1986-87 *In der Arche ist der Wurm drin (Something's Fishy on the Ark)*

The cartoon adventures of a wood-worm family on Noah's Ark.

Dir.: Wolfgang Urchs.
SP.: Wolfgang Urchs.
Cam.: Pierre Salvagnac, Helmut Müller, Christoph Beyer, Sebastian Schwerte, Roland Coulon.
Mus.: Frank Pleyer.
Prod.: MS-Film/Paramound/ Artemis.
81 min.

1986 *In der Wüste (In the Desert)*

Twenty-four hours in the life of two unemployed foreigners in Berlin, who sell their blood to finance a day of fun.

Dir.: Rafael Fuster-Pardo.

SP.: Horst Stasiak, from a story by Antonio Skarmeta.
Cam.: Rafael Fuster-Pardo.
Prod.: Deutsche Film- und Fernsehakademie Berlin.
Act.: Claudio Caceres Molina, Mustafa Saygili, Adriana
Altaras, Maric Temucin.
74 min.

1988-89 *In meinem Herzen, Schatz* (*In My Heart, Darling*)

Partly documentary hommage to the great German actor Hans
Albers.
Dir.: Hans-Christoph Blumenberg.
SP.: Hans-Christoph Blumenberg.
Cam.: Jörg Schmidt-Reitwein.
Mus.: Gerd Bellmann, Hans P. Ströer.
Prod.: Ottokar Runze Filmprod./ZDF.
Act.: Ulrich Tukur, Anette Kremer, Ilse Werner,
Bernhard Weber,
83 min.

1987 *Jacob hinter der blauen Tür* *(Jacob Behind the Blue Door)*

After the accidental death of his father, a twelve-year-old boy withdraws from those he loves, until he comes in contact with a down-and-out musician.

Dir.: Haro Senft.
SP.: Josef Rölz, Sylvia Ulrich, Horst Matouch, Haro Senft, Christina Reiner-Gum.
Cam.: Wedigo von Schultzendorff.
Mus.: David Knopfler.
Prod.: Alpha/ZDF.
Act.: Thomas Spielberg, Dagmar Deisen, Siegfried Kernen, Marquard Bohm, R. Roland.
96 min. (16mm)

1987 *Jäger der Engel* *(Hunter of Angels)*

The story of a lonely police detective who finds himself in a personal and professional conflict of interest when he falls in love with an "angel" whose actions are anything but angelic.

Dir.: Paris Kosmidis.
SP.: Paris Kosmidis.
Cam.: Wolfgang Dickmann.
Mus.: Ingfried Hoffmann.
Prod.: Oase/ProjectWDR.
Act.: Michael König, Ingo Hülsmann, Peter Roggisch, Anneliese Römer, Christiane Ostermayer.
90 min.

1984/6 *Jannan - die Abschiebung* *(Jannan - the Deportation)*

A Kurdish man flees Turkey and hopes to find a better life in West Germany. But once there, he runs up against gangsters, corrupt police and a hardened bureaucracy. He is supposed to be extradited back to Turkey, but commits suicide instead.

| | |
|---|---|
| Dir.: | Tim van Beveren. |
| SP.: | Renate Debus, Tim van Beveren. |
| Cam.: | Amir Ismail, Franz Schoys. |
| Mus.: | Georg Danzer, Roberto Fulvi, Franco Santucci, etc. |
| Prod.: | Spot. |
| Act.: | Yves Baron, Franz Nagel, Uwe-Karsten Koch, Hans-Gerd Kilbinger, Christiane Beihl. |
| 102 min. | |

1988  *Jenseits von Blau  (Beyond Blue)*

Using tenderness and music, a girl tries to get through to a young boy in a coma.

| | |
|---|---|
| Dir.: | Christoph Eichhorn. |
| SP.: | Michael Laux. |
| Cam.: | Hans-Günther Bücking. |
| Mus.: | Manfred Schoof. |
| Prod.: | Carsten Krüger Film und Fernsehproduktion/ E.M.L./Helmuth Costard Filmprod./Dibs-Film/D. Schubert. |
| Act.: | Sarah Jane Denalane, Karin Boyd, Peter Sattmann, Wolf Roth, Ingrid van Bergen. |
| 85 min. | |

1986  (German-Italian)  *Joan Lui  (Joan Lui)*

An unknown singer becomes a world-renowned rock star and preaches against all the evil in the world.

| | |
|---|---|
| Dir.: | Adriano Celentano. |
| SP.: | Adriano Celentano. |
| Cam.: | Alfio Contini. |
| Mus.: | Adriano Celentano. |

Prod.:   Extrafilm/C.G. Silver Film.
Act.:    Adriano Celentano, Marthe Keller, Federica Moro,
         Edwin Marian, Claudia Mori.
113 min.

1986 (Austrian-GDR-German)  *Johann Strauss - Der König ohne
Krone  (Johann Strauss - King without a Crown)*

The story of the waltz and operetta composer's loves and marriage.

Dir.:    Franz Antel.
SP.:     Frederic Morton, Tom W. Priman, Carl Szokoll,
         Georg Kovary, Klaus Eidam, Franz Antel.
Cam.:    Hans Matula.
Mus.:    Johann Strauss.
Prod.:   Johann Strauss-Film/DEFA/Toro/Video TTR.
Act.:    Oliver Tobias, Mary Crosby, Audrey Landers,
         Matthieu Carriere, Hugh Foster.
113 min.

1988-89 (German-French)  *Johanna d'Arc of Mongolia*

A group of wealthy people travel on the Trans-Siberian railroad at
the turn of the century; seven women are kidnapped in Mongolia and
get to know the life-styles and rituals of the natives there.

Dir.:    Ulrike Ottinger.
SP.:     Ulrike Ottinger.
Cam.:    Ulrike Ottinger.
Mus.:    Wilhelm Dieter Siebert.
Prod.:   Ulrike Ottinger/Popolar-Film/ZDF/La Sept.
Act.:    Delphine Seyrig, Irm Hermann, Gillian Scalici, Ines
         Sastre, Peter Kern.
165 min.

1987 *Johnny Flash*

Comedy about an electrician who becomes a pop star by singing silly
songs.

Dir.:   Werner Nekes.
SP.:    Werner Nekes, Peter Ritz.
Cam.:   Bernd Upnmoor, Serge Roman.
Mus.:   Helge Schneider.
Prod.:  Werner Nekes Filmprod.
Act.:   Helge Schneider, Andreas Kunze, Heike Melba-
        Fendel, Marianne Traub.
80 min.

1986  *Der Joker  (The Joker)*

A big city police detective, disgusted with his job, investigates a group
of violent crimes and seeks revenge on the organizations that sponsor
murder and drug dealing.

Dir.:   Peter Patzak.
SP.:    Peter Patzak, Jonathan Carroll.
Cam.:   Igor Luther, Dietrich Lohmann.
Mus.:   Peter Maffay.
Prod.:  K.S. Film/CTV/Lisa.
Act.:   Peter Maffay, Tahne Walsh, Elliott Gould, Michael
        York, Armin Mueller-Stahl.
97 min.

1988  *Die Jungfrauenmaschine  (The Virgin Machine)*

A young female journalist researches the topic "Romantic Love as
Woman's Illness," and comes to realize her own sexual identity
through her experiences with lesbians.

Dir.:   Monika Treut.
SP.:    Monika Treut.
Cam.:   Elfi Mikesch.
Mus.:   Mona Mur, Laibach, Blazing Hearts, Redheads,
        Pearl Harbour.
Prod.:  Hyäne Film I/II/NDR.
Act.:   Ina Blum, Marcelo Uriona, Dominique Gaspar,
        Susie Sexpert, Gad Klein.

## 1986  *Die Kameliendame  (The Camelia Lady)*

The famous and fateful love story of the "Camelia Lady" of Paris
from the novel by Alexandre Dumas.

Dir.:  John Neumeier.
SP.:  John Neumeier.
Cam.:  Ingo Hamer.
Mus.:  Frederic Chopin.
Prod.:  Polyphon.
Act.:  Marcia Haydee, Ivan Liska, Francois Klaus, Colleen
Scott, Vladimir Klos.
129 min.

## 1989  *Der Kameramann  (The Camera Man)*

A camera man has had no great professional success since his wife
left him. He tries everything to make the big breakthrough, then he
meets the little daughter of a porn-film actress and gets drawn into
her life.

Dir.:  Nikolai Karo.
SP.:  Edgar von Cossart.
Cam.:  Johannes Kollmann.
Mus.:  Peter Zwetkoff.
Prod.:  SWF/BR.
Act.:  Dieter Kirchlechner, Margit Geißler, Vera
Lünenschloß, Jan-Paul Biczycki, Jürgen Vogel.
82 min.

## 1985  *Kaminsky*

A combination of events leads to violence on the part of an

experienced policeman assigned to a remote station.

Dir/SP.: Michael Lähn.
Cam.:    Jörg Seidl.
Mus.:    Roberto C. Detree.
Prod.:   Panorama Film, Berlin/Deiniger & Stumpf.
Act.:    Klaus Löwitsch, Hannelore Elsner, Beate Finckh,
         Alexander Rudszun.
90 min.

1987 *Die Katze* *(The Cat)*

Thriller in which a calculating, clever gangster orchestrates a bank
robbery with hostages from his hotel room.

Dir.:    Dominik Graf.
SP.:     Uwe Erichsen, Christoph Fromm, from a novel by
         Uwe Erichsen.
Cam.:    Martin Schäfer.
Mus.:    Andreas Köbner.
Prod.:   Bavaria/ZDF.
Act.:    Götz George, Gudrun Landgrebe, Joachim
         Kemmer, Heinz Hoenig, Ralf Richter.
118 min.

1987 *Katzenjammer Kids*

Two young Germans search for father figures and idols on the road
between New York and Chicago.

Dir.:    Waltraud Ehrhardt.
SP.:     Waltraud Ehrhardt.
Cam.:    Diethard Prengel.
Mus.:    Etoile Dakar.
Prod.:   relief-Film/SWF.
Act.:    Ravi Karmalker, Angela Fischer, Thomas Dorff,
         Willy Tjan, Lotto Andor.
89 min.

## 1987 *Kiebich und Dutz (Kiebich and Dutz)*

Kiebich and Dutz live in a cave; Kiebich dreams of adventures, while the fearful Dutz refuses to leave his refuge. But when Kiebich gets into danger on one of his adventures, Dutz has to pull himself together and go out and rescue his friend.

Dir.:  F. K. Wächter.
SP.:  F. K. Wächter, from his play.
Cam.:  David Slama.
Mus.:  Jacques Zwart.
Prod.:  Salina/SFB/BR.
Act.:  Michael Altmann, Heinz Kraehkamp.
88 min.

## 1986 *Kies (Gravel)*

A small-time car thief falls in love with the daughter of a gravel pit owner.

Dir.:  Douglas Wolfsperger.
SP.:  Douglas Wolfsperger, based on an idea of Richard Gandor's.
Cam.:  Volker Maria Arend.
Mus.:  Charles Kalman.
Prod.:  Steinbock-Film.
Act.:  Hans Grafl, Ilse Matheis, Richard Gandor, Dorothea Moritz.
90 min.

## 1988 *Killing Blue*

While investigating the murder of a drug addict, a disillusioned police detective discovers that his best friend is a psychopathic killer.

Dir.:  Peter Patzak.
SP.:  Julia Kent, Paul Nicholas, Peter Patzak.
Cam.:  Anton Peschke.
Mus.:  Carl Carlton, Bertram Engel.

Prod.:   Lisa/K.S./Roxy.
Act.:    Armin Mueller-Stahl, Morgan Fairchild, Michael
         York, Frank Stallone, Julia Kent.
96 min.

1985  *Killing Cars*

Ralph Korda, an automobile designer, constructs a car that needs no
gas; he soon encounters difficulties in the company, however, and his
"Worldcar" is put on ice - indefinitely.

Dir/SP:  Michael Verhoeven.
Cam.:    Jacques Steyn.
Mus.:    Spliff.
Prod.:   Sentana-Film.
Act.:    Jürgen Prochnow, Senta Berger, Agnes Soral,
         Bernhard Wicki, Daniel Gelin, Stefan Meinke,
         William Conrad.
120 min.

1988  *Killing Drugs (Bangkok Story)*

A German development advisor in Thailand gets caught between the
drug bosses, the Thai police and the anti-drug department of the
German Federal Bureau of Investigation.

Dir.:    Rolf von Sydow.
SP.:     Rolf von Sydow, from a novel by Detlef
         Blettenberg.
Cam.:    Zoltan David.
Mus.:    Cong Su, Birger Heymann.
Prod.:   Manfred Durniok Prod./BR.
Act.:    Heiner Lauterbach, Günther Maria Halmer,
         Christine Garner, Rolf Hoppe, Joachim Bliese.
110 min.

1986  *Kinder aus Stein  (Children of Stone)*

An attractive model and her three men: She has a relationship with a small-time criminal, is in love with his roommate who washes dishes for a living, yet can't seem to let go of a photographer who is in love with her.

Dir.: Volker Maria Arend, Richard Claus.
SP.: Volker Maria Arend, Harald Göckeritz.
Cam.: David Slama, Reinhard Köchner.
Mus.: Norbert J. Schneider.
Prod.: Demos/NDR/WDR.
Act.: Claud Oliver Rudolph, Natja Brunkhorst, Uwe Fellensiek, Gunter Berger, Jürgen Vogel.
87 min.

1985 *King Kongs Faust (King Kong's Fist)*

A filmmaker sets out to find the unknown director of an old German film that received rave reviews at the 1984 Berlin Film Festival.

Dir.: Heiner Stadler.
SP.: Heiner Stadler, Ulrich Enzensberger, Lilly Targownik.
Cam.: Heiner Stadler, Markus Dürr.
Prod.: Katrin Seybold/NDR/Independent Feature Project, New York.
Act.: Leonhard Lansink, Werner Grassmann, Heinz van Houhuys, Wolfgang Längsfeld, Wim Wenders, Peter Przygodda, Helmut Färber, Franz Seitz, Laslo Benedek.
80 min.

1986-87 *Kismet, Kismet*

Two Turkish youths in Berlin develop in very different directions. The one sells carpets made by his relatives in Turkey and hopes to save enough money to make a movie. The other, who has been raised quite strictly, runs away and ends up in the drug and prostitution scene.

Dir.: Ismet Elci.

SP.:     Ismet Elci.
Cam.:    Albert Kittler.
Mus.:    Albert Kittler.
Prod.:   Ararat Medienproduktion und Vertrieb GmbH,
         Berlin.
Act.:    Ismet Elci, Alisan Keziban, Lothar Lambert,
         Wieland Speck, Ulrike S.
75 min.

1989   (German-French-English)   *Die Klage der Kaiserin   (The
Queen's Complaint)*

A series of collage-like scenes, put together by Pina Bausch's dance
troupe.

Dir.:    Pina Bausch.
SP.:     Pina Bausch.
Cam.:    Martin Schäfer, Detler Erler.
Mus.:    Matthias Burkert.
Prod.:   Wuppertaler Bühnen/ZDF/L'Arche Editeur/La
         Sept/Channel Four.
Act.:    Mariko Aoyama, Anne Marie Benati, Rolando
         Brenes Calvo, Antonio Carallo, Mechthild
         Grossmann.
95 min.

1986   *Der kleine Staatsanwalt   (The Little Attorney)*

A district attorney and a female police detective manage to gather
enough evidence to bring a white-collar criminal to trial, but the state
steps in and forces them to drop the case.

Dir.:    Hark Bohm.
SP.:     Hark Bohm.
Cam.:    Klaus Brix.
Mus.:    Jean "Toots" Thielemans, Herb Geller.
Prod.:   Hamburger Kino-Kompanie/NDR.
Act.:    Hark Bohm, Martin Lüttge, Corinna Harfouch,
         Michael Gwisdek, Alexander Radzun.

93 min.

1985 *Kokain - Das Tagebuch der Inga L.* (*Cocaine: The Diary of Inga L.*)

A small-time drug dealer dreams of moving up in the drug scene, brutally using his girlfriend to achieve this end.

Dir.:   R. Sharon.
Prod.:  Günter Schlesinger Filmprod.
Act.:   Renee Zaluski.
79 min.

1985 *Die Kolonie* (*The Colony*)

A father attempts to free his daughter from a German sect in South America, but runs up against lies, terror and despotism.

Dir.:   Orlando Lübbert.
SP.:    Kai Hermann.
Cam.:   Wolfgang Treu.
Mus.:   Inti Illimani.
Prod.:  Xenon-Film/WDR/HKK.
Act.:   Michael Degen, Grischa Huber, Elisabeth Degen, Eliana Cordova.
90 min.

1985 (German-Italian) *Kommando Leopard*

Rebels in a fictitious South American land battle the military government until their liberation movement is successful.

Dir.:   Anthony M. Dawson.
SP.:    Roy Nelson.
Cam.:   Peter Baumgartner.
Mus.:   Goran Kuzminac.
Prod.:  Ascot/Prestige.
Act.:   Lewis Collins, Klaus Kinski, Manfred Lehmann, Cristina Donadio, John Steiner.

103 min.

## 1987 *Komplizinnen* *(Accomplices)*

A young woman, in prison for bank robbery, works for cooperation among the women in the prison and thus achieves much needed reform.

Dir.:　Margit Czenki.
SP.:　Margit Czenki.
Cam.:　Hille Sagel.
Mus.:　Franz Hummel.
Prod.:　Elefant-Film/ZDF.
Act.:　Pola Kinski, Therese Affolter, Gerlinde Eger, Marianne Rosenberg, Ilse Page.
114 min.

## 1986 *Konzert für die rechte Hand* *(Concert for the Right Hand)*

A lonely park ranger takes a female window mannequin home, but loses her right arm on the way; a one-armed boutique owner finds it. When the ranger sets out to get the arm back, the arm develops a life of its own.

Dir.:　Michael Bartlett.
SP.:　Michael Bartlett.
Cam.:　Gerhardt Friedrich, Peter Kramm, Klaus Krieger.
Mus.:　Fernando Lafferiere.
Prod.:　Michael Bartlett.
Act.:　Miklos Königer, Sushila Day, Henry Akina, Ivo Kviring, Calvin Macherron.
82 min.

## 1989 *Kopffeuer*

A young Turkish woman, who is fleeing an arranged marriage, a Japanese musician, a political activist, and a male prostitute move into an abandoned dock building and gradually begin to understand and even like one another.

Dir.:     Erwin Michelberger.
SP.:      Erwin Michelberger.
Cam.:     Jörg Schalk.
Mus.:     Cyan.
Prod.:    LERM Film/NDR.
Act.:     Noguyuki Takayama, Klaus Pawalek, Seyran Ates,
          Ameise, Peter Kern.
87 min.

1988  (French-German)  *Der Krieg ist aus*  *(The War is Over)*

Two half brothers travel through France in 1944 trying to get to their
mother in Lyon. On the way, they come upon a wounded German
who was left behind by his outfit.

Dir.:     Jean-Loup Hubert.
SP.:      Jean-Loup Hubert.
Cam.:     Claude Lecomte.
Mus.:     Jürgen Knieper.
Prod.:    Camera Noire/TF 1/GPFI/Gerhard Schmidt Prod.
Act.:     Richard Bohringer, Antoine Hubert, Julien Hubert,
          Olivier Nembi, Isabelle Sadoyan.
105 min.

1985  *Der Krieg meines Vaters*  *(My Father's War)*

A young man begins to deal with the second World War and what it
has meant to his family when he reads a letter from his father.

Dir.:     Nico Hofmann.
SP.:      Nico Hofmann.
Cam.:     Ernst Kubitza.
Prod.:    Novoskop/HFFM.
Act.:     Hans Joachim Grau, Gabriele Badura, Heiner
          Kollhoff, Mathias Kopfmüller, Erika Kirchgässner.
60 min.

1985  *Küken für Kairo*  *(A Chick for Cairo)*

Two pilots find a stowaway baby chick on their plane, which leads to much excitement and several funny situations.

Dir.: Arend Agthe.
SP.: Monika Seck-Aghte, Arend Agthe.
Cam.: F. K. Koschnick.
Mus.: Matthias Rauhe, Martin Cyrus.
Prod.: Topas/WDR.
Act.: Hans Berrhenke, Karl-Friedrich Praetorius, Timmo Niesner, Lotti Huber.
75 min.

1985  *Die Küken kommen (Soldier Boys on the Loose)*

Six young men, just out of the Army, are hampered by their girl friends when they try to have some fun in Munich.

Dir/SP: Raoul Sternberg.
Cam.: Bernd Neubauer.
Prod.: Starfilm/Mutoskop/Lisa/Raphaela-Film.
Act.: Mark Altner, Frank Meyer-Brockmann, Hans Schödl, Joachim Bernhardt, Andreas Sprotelli.
92 min.

1985  *Die Kümmeltürkin geht (The Turkish Spice Lady is Leaving)*

A Turkish woman returns to her homeland after living in Berlin for fourteen years.

Dir/SP: Jeanine Meerapfel.
Cam.: Johann Feindt.
Mus.: Jakob Lichtmann.
Prod.: Journal Film.
Act.: Melek Tez, Familie Kantemir, Erna Krause, Etta Czach, Niyazi Türgay.
88 min.

1986  *Kunyonga - Mord in Afrika (Kunyonga - Murder in Africa)*

The son of a wealthy Berlin industrialist is sentenced to life in prison in Kenya, even though he's innocent. A black American reporter and Vietnam vet solves the case and arranges the son's freedom.

| | |
|---|---|
| Dir.: | Hubert Frank. |
| SP.: | Julia Furisch, Ron Williams. |
| Cam.: | Franz X. Lederle. |
| Mus.: | Gerhard Heinz. |
| Prod.: | Lisa/K.S. |
| Act.: | Ron Williams, Julia Kent, Christoph Eichhorn, Drew Lucas, Paul Breitner. |
| 91 min. | |

1988  *Der Kuß des Tigers  (Kiss of the Tiger)*

An au pair in Paris gets involved with a stranger who turns out to be a pathological murderer.

| | |
|---|---|
| Dir.: | Petra Haffter. |
| SP.: | Gerd Weiß, Petra Haffter, Peter Reinholz, from a novel by Francis Ryck. |
| Cam.: | Wolfgang Simon, Gerard Vendenberg. |
| Mus.: | Inga Humpe, Thomas Fehlmann. |
| Prod.: | Futura/Pro-ject/Filmedis. |
| Act.: | Beate Jensen, Stephane Ferrera, Yves Beneyton, Gunter Berger, Kristina van Eyck. |
| 104 min. | |

1988 *Land der Väter, Land der Söhne (Land of the Fathers, Land of the Sons)*

A young journalist researches his father's life, only to discover that during World War II, his father ran a factory in Poland and used concentration camp prisoners.

Dir.: Nico Hofmann.
SP.: Nico Hofmann.
Cam.: Laszlo Kadar.
Mus.: Peter Zwetkoff.
Prod.: B.A. Film/Nico Hofmann Filmprod./SWF/BR.
Act.: Karl-Heinz von Liebezeit, Katharina Meinecke, Lieselotte Rau, Adolf Laimböck, Wolf-Dietrich Sprenger.
89 min.

1990 *Land in Sicht (Land in Sight)*

A young girl spends her vacation at a horse farm in Schleswig-Holstein and comes to terms with many of her adolescent feelings.

Dir.: Berno Kürten.
SP.: Berno Kürten.
Cam.: Martin Gressmann.
Mus.: Hanno Rinne.
Prod.: Thilo von Arnim Filmprod./NDR.
Act.: Alexandra Schalaudeck, Aram Coen, Theo Gostischa, Hans-Peter Hallwachs, Dorothea Kaiser.
89 min.

1986 *Laputa*

A French architect and a female Polish photographer have been meeting for some time in Berlin to carry on their relationship, but neither is capable of making a firm commitment to the other. They end their relationship after a vehement argument.

Dir.:   Helma Sanders-Brahms.
SP.:    Helma Sanders-Brahms.
Cam.:   Eberhard Geick.
Mus.:   Matthias Meyer, Frederic Chopin.
Prod.:  Von Vietinghoff Filmprod.
Act.:   Sami Frey, Krystyna Janda.
92 min.

1989 (German-Hungarian) *Laurin*

In an idyllic harbor village at the turn of the century, a nine-year-old girl discovers a homosexual murderer and sets a trap for him. Horror.

Dir.:   Robert Sigl.
SP.:    Adam Rozgonyi, Robert Sigl.
Cam.:   Nyika Jancso.
Mus.:   Jacques Zwart, Hans Jansen.
Prod.:  Salinas/TS-Film/SWF/Dialog Studio.
Act.:   Dora Szinetar, Brigitte Karner, Karoly Eperjes, Heidi Temessy, Endre Katay.
84 min.

1985 *Lebe kreuz und sterbe quer  (Live and Die Wild)*

A good-natured baker is constantly being taken advantage of by the "good" citizens of his small town. When he fakes his own death, he reveals their greed and insensitivity, but it costs him his life.

Dir.:   Douglas Wolfsperger.
SP.:    Douglas Wolfsperger.
Cam.:   Karl Walter Lindenlaub.
Mus.:   Thomas Eichenbrenner.
Prod.:  Steinbock-Film.

Act.: Richard Gander, Luise Deschauer, Hans Grafl, Rudolf Waldemar Brem, Tobias Engelsing.
80 min.

1985 (German-Italian) *Leidenschaften (The Berlin Affair)*

A love triangle between an official in the Foreign Ministry in Berlin, his wife and the daughter of the Japanese ambassador ends in death for the man and the Japanese woman.

Dir.: Liliana Cavani.
SP.: Liliana Cavani, Roberta Mazzoni, from a novel by Junichiro Tanizaki.
Cam.: Dante Spinotti.
Mus.: Pino Donaggio.
Prod.: Nuova Kinofilm Cannon/KF.
Act.: Gudrun Landgrebe, Kevin McNally, Mio Takaki, Hanns Zischler, Massimo Girotti.
121 min.

1986 *Let's Go Crazy*

Detective comedy in which a group of young people, who have lost all their money in the casinos on the Riviera, decide to rob a bank. They get assistance from an elderly contessa who owns a theater next to the bank.

Dir.: Giorgio Christallini.
SP.: Joseph Breitenbach.
Cam.: Guglielmo Mancori.
Prod.: Podium Films.
Act.: Conrad Caster, Jenny Jürgens, Werner Pochath, Krista Söderbaum.
86 min.

1988 *Letzte Ausfahrt Brooklyn (Last Exit Brooklyn)*

In Brooklyn in 1952, a union strike sets off a series of brutal acts.

Dir.:    Uli Edel.
SP.:     Desmond Nakano, from a novel by Hubert Selby.
Cam.:    Stefan Czapsky.
Mus.:    Mark Knopfler.
Prod.:   Neue Constantin/Bavaria/Allied Filmmakers.
Act.:    Stephan Lang, Jennifer Jason Leigh, Burt Young,
         Peter Dobson, Jerry Orbach.
103 min.

1986  *Die Liebesschule der Josefine Mutzenbacher*  *(Josefine
Mutzenbacher's Love Academy)*

Josefine Mutzenbacher, a Viennese prostitute, inherits a villa from a
wealthy customer on the condition that she establish a love academy
there. Soft-porn.

Dir.:    Hans Billian.
SP.:     Hans Billian.
Cam.:    I. Steam.
Prod.:   Hit Film.
Act.:    Desiree Bernardy, Stacey Donovan, Jeanny Pepper,
         Jill Oliver.
85 min.

1987  *Linie 1 (Line 1)*

A young woman from the provinces comes to Berlin to look for her
boyfriend; she gets involved with the Berlin subculture, but also meets
some "average" Berliners as well.

Dir.:    Reinhard Hauff.
SP.:     Volker Ludwig, Reinhard Hauff, from a stage
         musical by the Berlin Grips-Theater.
Cam.:    Frank Brühne.
Mus.:    Birger Heymann.
Prod.:   Bioskop/WDR/SFB.
Act.:    Inka Groetschel, Ilona Schulz, Dieter Landuris,
         Thomas Ahrens, Petra Yieser.
99 min.

1983 *Lisa und die Riesen (Lisa and the Giants)*

A five-year-old girl who feels neglected by her parents flees into her own dreamworld.

|  |  |
|---|---|
| Dir.: | Thomas Draeger. |
| SP.: | Thomas Draeger. |
| Cam.: | Hille Sagel. |
| Mus.: | Graziano Mandozzi. |
| Prod.: | Cikon/ZDF. |
| Act.: | Eva Lebenheim, Sigfrit Steiner, Alexander Piele, Brigitte von Lersner, Kurt Schmidtchen. |

96 min.

1986 (German-American) *Lockwood Desert, Nevada*

A young, unemployed German man takes off to explore the U.S.A., goes through a period of bad luck but finally ends up happy.

|  |  |
|---|---|
| Dir.: | Hans Noever. |
| SP.: | Hans Noever. |
| Cam.: | Peter Gauhe. |
| Mus.: | Frank Loef. |
| Prod.: | Olga/BR/ORF. |
| Act.: | Tobias Hoesl, Henner Kuckuck, W.L. Schuh, Susan Beyer, Sal Provenza. |

81 min.

1988 (French-German) *Der Löwe (The Lion)*

A successful businessman decides to take a break from his routine, but shortly thereafter gets re-involved, along with a newly acquired, younger friend, in his business affairs, which have gone downhill in his absence.

|  |  |
|---|---|
| Dir.: | Claude Lelouch. |
| SP.: | Claude Lelouch. |
| Cam.: | Jean-Yves Le Mener. |
| Mus.: | Francis Lai. |

Prod.:  Films 13/Cerito Films/FT 1/Stallion/Gerhard
        Schmidt Film.
Act.:   Jean-Paul Belmondo, Richard Anconina, Marie-
        Sophie L., Jean-Philippe Chatrier, Daniel Gelin.
120 min.

1988 (Swiss-German) *Macao oder Die Rückseite des Meeres (Macao - or The Back Side of the Sea)*

A Swiss linguist and a pilot crash between Zürich and Stockholm and are presumed dead. However, they have been washed ashore in "Macao," a place that seems to be on the other end of the world.

Dir.: Clemens Klopfenstein.
SP.: Clemens Klopfenstein, Wolfram Groddeck, Felix Tissi.
Cam.: Clemens Klopfenstein.
Prod.: Ombra/SRG/Pandora/ZDF.
Act.: Max Rüdlinger, Christine Lauterburg, Hans-Dieter Jendreyko, Hans Rudolf Twerenbold, Che Tin Hong.
90 min.

1987 (French-German) *Macbeth*

Movie of the Verdi opera, done by the Bolognese Teatro Comunale.

Dir.: Claude D'Anna.
SP.: F.M. Piave, from the play by William Shakespeare.
Cam.: Pierre Dupouey.
Mus.: Giuseppe Verdi.
Prod.: Dedalus/SFPC/TF 1/Unitel.
Act.: Shirley Verrett, Leo Nucci, Johan Leysen, Samuel Rames, Philippe Volter, Veriano Luchette.
135 min.

1987 *Das Mädchen mit den Feuerzeugen (The Girl with the Cigarette Lighters)*

On Christmas Eve, four wheelchair-bound young people make off
with a sack of money that had been donated for their institute and go
off to have a night on the town in Munich. There, they encounter an
angel in the form of a cigarette-lighter vendor, and she grants them
three wishes.

> Dir.:   Ralf Huettner.
> SP.:    Andy Hoetzel, Ralf Huettner.
> Cam.:   Diethard Prengel.
> Mus.:   Andreas Köbner.
> Prod.:  Elan/Gieske & Co./ZDF.
> Act.:   Stefan Wood, Arnold Frühwald, Rupert Seidl,
>         Enrico Böttcher, Eva Ordonez.
> 105 min.

### 1986 *Der Madonna-Mann (Operation Madonna)*

An Australian geologist is a passenger on a flight that has to make
an unscheduled landing in Hamburg. Here, due to a case of
mistaken identity, he becomes entangled in a complicated plot
involving a killer and a gangster boss.

> Dir.:   Hans-Christoph Blumenberg.
> SP.:    Jonathan Thornhill, Hans-Christoph Blumenberg.
> Cam.:   Theo van de Sande.
> Mus.:   Manfred Schoof.
> Prod.:  Radiant/NDF.
> Act.:   Marius Müller-Westernhagen, Renee Soutendijk,
>         Michael Losndale, Heinrich Schweiger, Peter Kraus.
> 93 min.

### 1986 *Magic Sticks*

A drummer possesses magic drumsticks that inspire New Yorkers to
dance but get him into trouble with two gangsters.

> Dir.:   Peter Keglevic.
> SP.:    Christopher Ragazzo, George Kranz, Peter
>         Keglevic.

Cam.:  Edward Klosinski.
Mus.:  George Kranz.
Prod.:  Peter Keglevic Filmprod./Wolfang Odenthal Film/Monika Nüchtern Filmprod./WDR.
Act.:  George Kranz, Kelly Curtis, Chico Hamilton, David Margulies, Jack McGee.
91 min.

1987 *Man spricht deutsch (German spoken here)*

The last vacation day in sunny Italy for a Bavarian family is filled with events that show that they haven't overcome their ignorant prejudices against Italians. The film also shows each family member's fantasy about what he or she wishes would have happened on their vacation.

Dir.:  Hanns Christian Müller.
SP.:  Hanns Christian Müller, Gerhard Polt.
Cam.:  James Jacobs.
Mus.:  Hanns Christian Müller, diverse hits.
Prod.:  Vision/Maran/Solaris.
Act.:  Gerhard Polt, Gisela Schneeberger, Dieter Hildebrandt, Isa Haller, Pamela Prati.
84 min.

1985 (German-Philippine) *Manila Tatoo (Red Roses for a Callgirl)*

A German architect in Manila learns that his son is dying of leukemia, so he hires a callgirl to make his last weeks sweeter. The two fall in love, which enrages the girl's pimp.

Dir.:  Bobby A. Suarez.
Prod.:  Lisa/Bas Manila.
Act.:  Julia Kent, Werner Pocharth, Manfred Seipold, Maria Isabel Lopez, Robert Marius.
79 min.

1989-90 *Der Mann mit den Bäumen (The Man with the Trees)*

An elderly man tells his eight-year-old granddaughter of his
encounter with a French shepherd who had enriched the landscape
wherever he went by planting trees, thus also enriching the lives of
the land's inhabitants.

Dir.:   Werner Kubny.
SP.:    Werner Kubny, from a story by Jean Giono.
Cam.:   Werner Kubny.
Mus.:   Piet Klocke, Omar Kelaptrischwili.
Prod.:  Kubny Filmproduktion/WDR.
Act.:   Ferdinand Dux, Anna Ludwig, Franz Bulin,
        Wolfgang Kaven, Konstantin Graudus.
80 min.

1985 *Männer (Men)*

Comedy in which two men fight for the same woman.

Dir.:   Doris Dörrie.
SP.:    Doris Dörrie.
Cam.:   Helge Weindler.
Mus.:   Claus Bantzer.
Prod.:  Olga-Film/ZDF.
Act.:   Heiner Lauterbach, Uwe Ochsenknecht, Ulrike
        Kriener, Janna Marangosoff, Dietmar Bär.
99 min.

1988 (German-French) *Manöver (Maneuvers)*

Set in 1959, the film tells the story of a Lieutenant in the National
People's Army of the German Democratic Republic, who has the
assignment to recruit a secretary in the West German Ministry of
Defense. His task gets complicated when he falls in love with her.

Dir.:   Helma Sanders-Brahms.
SP.:    Helma Sanders-Brahms.
Cam.:   Claus Deubel.
Mus.:   Jürgen Knieper.
Prod.:  Helma Sanders-Filmproduktion/La Sept.

Act.: Adriana Altaras, Johannes Herrschmann, Alfred Edel, Elisabeth Zündel, Dominik Bender.
103 min.

1988 *Maria von den Sternen* (*Maria of the Stars*)

A fascinating young woman meets an unemployed teacher who moves into her neighborhood.

Dir.: Thomas Mauch.
SP.: Thomas Mauch.
Cam.: Thomas Mauch.
Mus.: Christoph Oliver.
Prod.: Thomas Mauch.
Act.: Katja Junge, Robert Duessler, Heiko Deutschmann, Michael Lot, Eric Schildkraut.
90 min.

1988 *Martha Jellneck*

An arthritic woman who is confined to her apartment discovers that the murderer of her brother is passing himself off as her brother, and she plans revenge on the ex-SS murderer.

Dir.: Kai Wessel.
SP.: Beate Langmaack.
Cam.: Achim Poulheim.
Mus.: Michael Haase.
Prod.: Ottokar Runze Filmprod.
Act.: Heidemarie Hatheyer, Dominique Horwitz, Angelika Thomas, Ulrich Matschoss, Hayati Yesilkaya.
93 min.

1989 (German-Italian) *Martha und ich* (*Martha and Me*)

The wife of a half-Jewish doctor in Prague refuses to divorce her husband--and save herself--when the Nazis take over their country in 1938.

Dir.:    Jiri Weiss.
SP.:     Jiri Weiss.
Cam.:    Viktor Ruzicka.
Mus.:    Jiri Stivin.
Prod.:   Iduna Film/Progefi/TF 1 Film Prod./ZDF/Canal
         Plus/RAI 2.
Act.:    Marianne Sägebrecht, Michel Piccoli, Vaclav
         Chalupa, Ondrej Vetchy, Jana Altmanova, Klaus
         Grünberg.
107 min.

1986 (Finnish-French-German-English) *Maschenka*

A young Russian nobleman emigrates to Berlin, where he discovers
that his neighbor's wife, who still lives in Russia, was his first love.

Dir.:    John Goldschmidt.
SP.:     John Mortimer, from a novel by Vladimir Nabokov.
Cam.:    Wolfgang Treu.
Mus.:    Nikolaus Glowna.
Prod.:   Clasart, Jörn Donner/FR3/Channel Four/ORF.
Act.:    Cary Elwes, Irina Brook, Sunnyi Melles, Jonathan
         Coy, Freddie Jones.
103 min.

1986 *Meier*

Comedy in which a wallpaper specialist from East Berlin makes it big
in the business by importing wallpaper from the West.

Dir.:    Peter Timm.
SP.:     Peter Timm.
Cam.:    Klaus Eichhammer.
Mus.:    Peter Goldfuss.
Prod.:   pro-ject/Popular/Maran.
Act.:    Rainer Grenkowitz, Nadja Engelbrecht, Alexander
         Hauff, Thomas Bestvater, Rene Grams.
99 min.

1980 *Mein Gott, Didi!* *(My God, Didi!)*

Another in the series of Didi stories. This time he causes all kinds of confusion as a sales clerk in a sporting goods store.

Dir.: Ralf Gregan, Dieter Hallervorden.
SP.: Ralf Gregan, Dieter Hallervorden.
Prod.: Ufa/ZDF.
Act.: Dieter Hallervorden, Rotraud Schindler, Peter Schiff, Ursula Heyer.
88 min.

1988 (Hungarian-German) *Mein 20. Jahrhundert* *(My Twentieth Century)*

A look at the unfulfilled hopes of the previous century in the twentieth century.

Dir.: Ildiko Enyedi.
SP.: Ildiko Enyedi.
Cam.: Tibor Mathe.
Mus.: Laszlo Vidovszky.
Prod.: Budapest Film-Studio Vallalat/Mafilm/Friedländer Filmprod.
Act.: Dorota Segda, Oleg Jankowski, Peter Andorai, Gabor Mathe, Paulus Manker.
103 min.

1926/1984 (German/American) *Metropolis*

A modernized, colorized version of Fritz Lang's 1926 silent classic about the dramatic events in a futuristic, totalitarian society where machines are more important than people. Includes a new music track by Moroder.

Dir.: Fritz Lang (Giorgio Moroder).
SP.: Thea von Harbou.
Cam.: Karl Freund, Günther Rittau.
Mus.: Giorgio Moroder.

Prod.:   Ufa (Giorgio Moroder Enterprises/PSO).
Act.:    Gustav Fröhlich, Brigitte Helm, Alfred Abel, Rudolf
         Klein-Rogge, Heinrich George.
80 min.

1985  *Miko - Aus der Gosse zu den Sternen  (From the Gutter to the Stars)*

The rise of the Berlin rock singer named Miko.

Dir.:    Frank Ripploh.
SP.:     Frank Ripploh.
Cam.:    Rudolf Blahacek.
Mus.:    Miko.
Prod.:   Frank Ripploh Filmprod./Radio Bremen.
Act.:    Petra Mikolajczak (= Miko), Frank Ripploh,
         Tamara Kafka, Zak Preen, Eric Steinmetz.
100 min.

1987-88  *Das Mikroskop  (The Microscope)*

Comedy about a couple in which the woman wants to get married
and have children, but the man doesn't want to get "tied down."

Dir.:    Rudolf Thome.
SP.:     Rudolf Thome.
Cam.:    Martin Schäfer.
Mus.:    Hanno Rinne.
Prod.:   Moana-Film.
Act.:    Vladimir Weigl, Adriana Altaras, Malgoscha Gebel,
         Alexander Malkowski, Barbara Beutler.
97 min.

1987 (German-Italian)  *Mira*

An Italian city serves as the "leading lady" in this film, which attempts
to establish her identity based on her factual as well as her mythical
past.

Dir.:     Silvana Abbrescia-Rath.
SP.:      Silvana Abbrescia-Rath.
Cam.:     Helmut-Ulrich Weiss.
Mus.:     Süelözgen Engin, Hüseyin Kaynarcali, Ciccio & Cola.
Prod.:    DFFB.
Act.:     Claudia Ghirardelli, Guia Principali, Gianvito Spizzico, Mariano Brescia, Giacomo Principalli.
96 min. (16 mm)

1989 *Mix Wix*

The owner of the Munich department store, Mix Wix, turns more and more to the teachings of oriental religions, and after much consideration, gives his empire to his employees.

Dir.:     Herbert Achternbusch.
SP.:      Herbert Achternbusch.
Cam.:     Adam Olech, Hermann Fahr.
Prod.:    Herbert Achternbusch Prod.
Act.:     Herbert Achternbusch, Monika Lemberger, Waggie Brömse, Alfred Edel, Annamirl Bierbichler.
88 min.

1985-86 (German-Italian) *Momo*

Movie of Michael Ende's novel, in which a small, peaceful, idyllic community is threatened by time thieves.

Dir.:     Johannes Schaaf.
SP.:      Johannes Schaaf, Rosemarie Fendel, Marcello Coscio, Michael Ende, from the novel by Michael Ende.
Cam.:     Xaver Schwarzenberger.
Mus.:     Angelo Branduardi.
Prod.:    Rialto/Iduna/S.A.C.I.S./Cinecitta.
Act.:     Radost Bokel, Mario Adorf, Armin Mueller-Stahl, Sylvester Groth, Leopoldo Trieste.
104 min.

1989  *Mondjäger  (Moon Hunters)*

Fourteen-year-old Katrin searches in the Brazilian jungle for the
cause of the plane crash that killed her father. In doing so, she
stumbles upon a plot to massacre the natives there.

Dir.:   Jens-Peter Behrend.
SP.:   Jens-Peter Behrend, Elfie Donnelly, from a novel by
       Sigrid Heuck.
Cam.:  Adrian Cooper, Carsten Krüger.
Mus.:  Jürgen Knieper.
Prod.:  Carsten Krüger Film- und Fernsehproduktion/SFB.
Act.:  Marie Bierstedt, Karl Michael Vogler, Agnelo
      Temrite-Wadzatse, Murilo Alvarenga, Sabine
      Kotzur.
90 min.

1989  *Moon 44*

In the year 2038, all the raw materials on Earth have been used up,
and battle lines are being drawn for the "possession" of raw materials
in space. On one planet, which is being used for mining as well as
for incarcerating dangerous criminals, a conflict arises between a
security guard and a crooked warden.

Dir.:   Roland Emmerich.
SP.:   Dean Heyde, Roland Emmerich.
Cam.:  Karl Walter Lindenlaub.
Mus.:  Joel Goldsmith.
Prod.:  Centropolis.
Act.:  Michael Pare, Lisa Eichhorn, Malcolm MacDowell,
      Brian Thompson, Leon Rippy.
98 min.

1988 (German-Austrian) *Nachsaison* *(Off-Season)*

A young masseur gets a job in a new hotel in the forsaken resort town of Badgastein, but fails in his attempt to restore order to his life.

Dir.: Wolfram Paulus.
SP.: Wolfram Paulus.
Cam.: Christian Berger.
Mus.: Bert Breit.
Prod.: Voissfilm/BR/Marwo.
Act.: Albert Paulus, Günther Halmer, Daniela Obermeir, Mercedes Echerer, Joanna Paulus.
88 min.

1985 *Die Nacht (The Night)*

A two-part, six-hour-long film with only one actress; a lament for Europe, according to the director.

Dir.: Hans Jürgen Syberberg.
Cam.: Xaver Schwarzenberger.
Mus.: Bach, Wagner.
Act.: Edith Clever.
360 min.

1987 *Die Nacht des Marders (The Night of the Marten)*

A young farm woman in Lower Bavaria falls victim to the attractive powers of an apparently dumb stranger; when she can no longer resist him, the evil begins.

Dir.: Maria Teresia Wagner.

105

SP.:     Maria Teresia Wagner.
Cam.:    Wedigo von Schultzendorff.
Mus.:    Rainer Fabich.
Prod.:   Alpha-Film Augele/Hans-Jürgen Seybusch, Gesell-
         schaft für Werbung und Produktion/WDR.
Act.:    Annamirl Bierbichler, Franz Buchrieser, Claus
         Eberth, Herta Böhm-Wildner, Nini von Quast.
94 min.

1989 (Italian-French-German) *Nachtsonne (Night Sun)*

Bitterly disappointed by love in 18th-century Italy, a young soldier
flees into a monastery, then lives as a hermit in the mountains until
temptation catches up with him.

Dir.:    Paolo Taviani, Vittorio Taviani.
SP.:     Paolo Taviani, Vittorio Taviani, Tonino Guerra,
         from a story by Leo Tolstoy.
Cam.:    Giuseppe Lanci.
Mus.:    Nicola Piovani.
Prod.:   Filmtre/RAI Uno/Capoul/Interpool/Sara/Direkt
         Film/ZDF.
Act.:    Julian Sands, Charlotte Gainsbourg, Massimo
         Bonetti, Nastassja Kinski, Margarita Lozano.
113 min.

1985 (German-Austrian-Yugoslavian) *Nägel mit Köpfen (Vier
Männer und ein Kamel) (Four Men and a Camel)*

An art student gets thrown in jail because of a loan shark, but gets
revenge later by selling the loan shark counterfeit art.

Dir.:    Wigbert Wicker.
SP.:     Wigbert Wicker.
Cam.:    Walter Kinler.
Mus.:    Roland Baumgartner.
Prod.:   Hanspeter Meier Filmprod./Intertel
         Television/Jadran/HR.
Act.:    Rainer Grenkowitz, Susanne Herletz, Heinz

Reincke, Klausjürgen Wussow, Karl Lieffen.
90 min.

**1985-86 (German-Italian-French) *Der Name der Rose* (*The Name of the Rose*)**

In the late Middle Ages (1327), a Franciscan Monk and his assistant unravel a series of murders in a Benedictine monastery in Northern Italy.

Dir.:   Jean-Jacques Annaud.
SP.:    Andrew Birkin, Gerard Brach, Howard Franklin, Alain Godard, from the novel by Umberto Eco.
Cam.:   Tonino Delli.
Mus.:   James Horner.
Prod.:  Neue Constantin/ZDF/Cristaldi/Films Ariane.
Act.:   Sean Connery, F. Murray Abraham, Feodor Chaliapin Jr., William Hickey, Michael Lonsdale, Christian Slater.
131 min.

**1986 (German-Ghana) *Nana Akoto***

The chief of a village in Central Ghana is old and tired, but still insists that his palace be finished at the expense of much needed cattle and water wells.

Dir.:   King Ampaw, Ingrid Mertner.
SP.:    King Ampaw, Elisabeth Jensen, David Kwame.
Cam.:   Volker Mach, Francis Adoboe.
Mus.:   Chris Bediako.
Prod.:  NDR/Reinery Verlag und Filmprod./Ghana Film Industry.
Act.:   Joe Eyison, Emmanuel Agbinowu, Osei Kwabena, Grace Nortey, Grace Ofoe.
94 min.

**1985 *Nessie, das verrückteste Monster der Welt* (*Nessie, the Craziest Monster in the World*)**

Some young mechanics use their imitation Loch Ness monster to save the occupants of a castle from a murder attempt.

Dir/SP: Rudolf Zehetgruber.
Cam.: Heinz Pehlke, Rüdiger Meichsner.
Mus.: Hans Hammerschmid.
Prod.: Barbara-Film.
Act.: Horst Niendorf, Gert Duwner, Ulli Kinalzik, Oliver Rohrbeck, Miriam und Delia Behpour, Britta Pohland.
83 min.

1990 *Neuner*

Tragicomedy in which a building contractor travels to Berlin to meet the sister of his deceased lover, upon which his wife leaves him for another man.

Dir.: Werner Masten.
SP.: Jurek Becker.
Cam.: Klaus Eichhammer.
Mus.: Klaus Doldinger.
Prod.: Nova Film.
Act.: Manfred Krug, Claudia Wedekind, Klaus Wennemann, Anni Sibylle Canonica, Peter Lohmeyer.
93 min.

1986 (German-Austrian) *News - Reise in eine strahlende Zukunft*

A British reporter discovers illegal dealings involving the disposal of atomic waste. After his disappearance, his lover, their daughter and a photographer search for him across the continents.

Dir.: Rainer Erler.
SP.: Rainer Erler.
Cam.: Wolfgang Grasshoff.
Mus.: Eugen Thomas.
Prod.: Reflex/Brooks & Film/ZDF/ORF.

Act.:   Birgitt Doll, Albert Fortell, Mark Lee, Kitty Myers,
        Lucia Bensasson.
126 min.

1985 *Nicht nichts ohne dich* (*Ain't Nothin' Without You*)

An ambitious female director of B-movies tries her hand at living in
an alternative setting with foreigners, but fails.

Dir.:   Pia Frankenberg.
SP.:    Pia Frankenberg.
Cam.:   Thomas Mauch.
Mus.:   Horst Mühlbradt.
Prod.:  Pia Frankenberg.
Act.:   Pia Frankenberg, Klaus Bueb, Alfred Edel, Adelina
        Almeida, Hark Bohm.
88 min.

1985 *Niemanns Zeit* (*Niemann's Time*)

A film that deals with the problem of coming to grips with the Nazi
past, as well as the "nature" of the German people.

Dir/SP: Horst Kurnitzky, Marion Schmid.
Cam.:   Wladimir Woitinski.
Mus.:   Jolyon Brettingham-Smith with the Studio Orchestra
        of Berlin.
Prod.:  Literarisches Colloquium, Berlin/WDR.
Act.:   Gerd Wameling, Elke Petri, Klaus Heinrich,
        Hansjörg Hemminger, Reinhold Messner, Bruno
        Kurz, Sira Manopas.
106 min.

1985 *Novemberkatzen* (*November Cats*)

A woman, whose husband has left her with four children, gets
spiritual and material help from her mother-in-law.

Dir.:   Sigrus Koeppe.

SP.:     Mirjan Pressler, Sigrun Koeppe, from a novel by
         Mirjan Pressler.
Cam.:    Volker Tittel.
Mus.:    Gunther Ress.
Prod.:   Quadriga/Tornesch/SWF.
Act.:    Angela Hunger, Ursela Monn, Katharina Brauren,
         Robert Zimmerling, Jürgen Vogel.
104 min.

1985  *Novembermond (November Moon)*

The story of November Messing, a German Jewess who managed to
stay alive in Paris through the Nazi occupation.

Dir/SP: Alexandra von Grote.
Cam.:    Bernard Zitzermann.
Mus.:    Egisto Macchi.
Prod.:   Ottokar Runze Filmprod./Sun 7 Prod., Paris.
Act.:    Gabriele Osburg, Christiane Millet, Danièle
         Delorme, Bruno Pradal, Stépane Garcin, Louise
         Martini, Gerhard Olschewski.
106 min.

## 1987  *Ödipussy*

Loriot tells the story of a 56-year-old "mama's boy" and his romantic relationship to a somewhat inhibited psychologist.

Dir.:    Loriot (Vicco von Bülow).
SP.:    Loriot.
Cam.:    Xaver Schwarzenberger.
Mus.:    Rolf Wilhelm.
Prod.:    Rialto/Bavaria.
Act.:    Loriot, Evelyn Hamann, Katharina Brauren, Edda Seippel, Richard Lauffen.
88 min.

## 1985  *Operation Dead End*

A team of scientists attempts to test the behaviour of three people in a radiation-proof house after an atomic incident; the two men and a woman are not able to complete the test.

Dir.:    Nikolai Müllerschön.
SP.:    Stanislav Barabas, Nikolai Müllerschön.
Cam.:    Jacques Steyn.
Mus.:    Jacques Zwart.
Prod.:    OKO/Dieter Geissler.
Act.:    Isabelle Willer, Uwe Ochsenknecht, Hannes Jaenicke, Günter Maria Halmer, Felix von Manteuffel.
95 min.

## 1984-85  *Orchideen des Wahnsinns (Orchids of Insanity)*

A young woman is the sole heir to her father's fortune after he is allegedly murdered and sees herself as the object of malicious attacks.

Dir.:    Nikolai Müllerschön.
SP.:     Eberhardt Weißbarth, Wolfgang Büld.
Cam.:    Stefan Motzek.
Mus.:    Jacques Zwart.
Prod.:   Extrafilm.
Act.:    Diana Körner, Peter von Strombeck, Krikar
         Melikyan, Andy Anderson, April de Luda.
79 min.

1978  (German-Italian-Spanish)  *Orgie des Todes*  (*Orgy of Death*)

An unconventional chief of police investigates a murder in a girls' boarding school and finds that one witness after the other is also killed.

Dir.:    Alberto Negri.
SP.:     Miguel de Echarri y Germundi, Franco Ferrini,
         Peter Berlin.
Cam.:    Carlo Carlini.
Prod.:   CCC/Daimo/Cipi.
Act.:    Christine Kaufmann, Fabio Testi, Ivan Desny.
78 min.

1987  *Ossegg oder Die Wahrheit über Hänsel und Gretel*  (*Ossegg or the Truth about Hansel and Gretel*)

Satire in which an archaeologist sets out to find and dig up the Ginger Bread House from the Grimm's fairy tale "Hänsel and Gretel."

Dir.:    Thees Klahn.
SP.:     Thees Klahn, from a book by Hans Traxler.
Cam.:    Lothar E. Stickelbrucks.
Mus.:    Janos Masik.
Prod.:   Dragon Cine/Studio Hamburg/WDR/HR.
Act.:    Jean-Pierre Leaud, Alfred Edel, Romy Haag, Klaus

Rohrmoser, Hark Bohm.
82 min.

### 1989  *Otto - Der Außerfriesische  (Otto out of Frisia)*

Comedian Otto Waalkes portrays a Frisian who lives in an abandoned lighthouse which is to be torn down for a rocket test site. Otto saves his home by joining ranks with his long-lost brother in Florida.

Dir.:   Otto Waalkes, Marijan Vajda.
SP.:    Bernd Eilert, Robert Gernhardt, Peter Knorr, Otto Waalkes.
Cam.:   Egon Werdin.
Mus.:   Thomas Kukuck, Christoph Leis-Bendorff.
Prod.:  Rialto/Rüssel Video & Audio.
Act.:   Otto Waalkes, Barbara May, Volkmar Kleinert, Hans-Peter Hallwachs, Wolfgang Zerlett.
92 min.

### 1985  *Otto - Der Film (Otto - The Movie)*

A naive young man from the country gets into the clutches of a loan shark in the big city, but manages to find his true love in the daughter of a nobleman.

Dir.:   Xaver Schwarzenberger, Otto Waalkes.
SP.:    Bernd Eilert, Robert Gernhardt, Peter Knorr, Otto Waalkes.
Cam.:   Xaver Schwarzenberger, Michael Stöger.
Mus.:   Herb Geller.
Prod.:  Rialto/Rüssl Video Audio.
Act.:   Otto Waalkes, Jessika Cardinahl, Elisabeth Wiedemann, Sky Dumont, Peter Kuiper.
85 min.

### 1987  *Otto - Der neue Film  (Otto - The New Movie)*

The comedian Otto Waalkes plays a helpless bumbler who lets

himself be terrorized by the super and also fails to win the affections of a beautiful woman.

Dir.:   Xaver Schwarzenberger, Otto Waalkes.
SP.:   Bernd Eilert, Robert Gernhardt, Peter Knorr, Otto Waalkes.
Cam.:   Xaver Schwarzenberger.
Mus.:   Thomas Kukuck, Christoph Leis-Bendorff.
Prod.:   Rialto/Rüssel/ZDF.
Act.:   Otto Waalkes, Ute Sander, Anja Jaenicke, Georg Blumensaat, Friedrich Schönfelder.
85 min.

### 1987 *Out of Rosenheim (Bagdad Cafe)*

A female tourist from Rosenheim is left behind by her husband after they quarrel in the middle of the California desert. She takes up residence in a shabby motel nearby and gradually wins the affection of everyone living there.

Dir.:   Percy Adlon.
SP.:   Percy Adlon, Eleonore Adlon.
Cam.:   Bernd Heinl.
Mus.:   Bob Telson.
Prod.:   Pelemele/Pro-ject/BR/HR.
Act.:   Marianne Sägebrecht, CCH Pounder, Jack Palance, Christine Kaufmann, Monica Calhoun.
108 min.

1988  (German-Czech)  *Pan Tau - der Film*  *(Pan Tau - the Movie)*

When the entire scenery for a science-fiction movie is destroyed, the director decides to make a children's movie using the rubble as background. For his leading role, he convinces an alcoholic actor to get his "act" together.

Dir.:   Jindrich Polak.
SP.:   Ota Hofman, Jindrich Polak.
Cam.:   Emil Sitorek.
Mus.:   Manfred Schoof.
Prod.:   Plaza-Tele FAZ/WDR/Filmové Studio Barrandov.
Act.:   Otto Simanek, Dana Vavrova, Ute Christensen, Jan Vlasak, Jakub Drocar.
93 min.

1986  *Paradies*  *(Paradise)*

In order to put some life into her marriage, a spoiled woman invites her girlhood friend to live with her and her husband, thereby also inviting catastrophe.

Dir.:   Doris Dörrie.
SP.:   Doris Dörrie.
Cam.:   Helga Heindler.
Mus.:   Claus Bantzer, Combo Cocktail.
Prod.:   Delta/WDR.
Act.:   Heiner Lauterbach, Katharina Thalbach, Sunnyi Melles, Hanne Wieder, Ernst-Erich Buder.
107 min.

1987  *Der Passagier - Welcome to Germany*

A successful Jewish film director from America attempts to ease his conscience by making a film in Germany about the circumstances surrounding an anti-Semitic Nazi film from 1942. He had been forced, along with other Jewish concentration camp prisoners, to act in the movie as an extra, and had been responsible for a friend's death through betrayal.

> Dir.:     Thomas Brasch.
> SP.:      Thomas Brasch.
> Cam.:    Axel Block.
> Mus.:    Günther Fischer.
> Prod.:    VonVietinghoff/Vietinghoff/RoadMovies/George-
>          Reinhard-Prod./ZDF/Channel Four.
> Act.:     Tony Curtis, Katharina Thalbach, Matthias Habich,
>          Alexandra Stewart, Charles Regnier.
> 102 min.

**1986   *Peng! Du bist tot! (The Microchip Killer) (Bang! You're Dead!)***

Comedy in which three people end up in a deadly game searching for a computer expert who can cause malicious accidents using microchips.

> Dir.:     Adolf Winkelmann.
> SP.:      Walter Kempley, Matthias Seelig.
> Cam.:    David Slama.
> Mus.:    Piet Klocke.
> Prod.:    Delta/WDR.
> Act.:     Ingolf Lück, Rebecca Pauly, Hermann Lause,
>          Volker Spengler, Rolf Zacher.
> 102 min.

**1988   (German-Hungarian)   *Peter im Wunderland (Peter in Wonderland)***

Two young Hungarian lovers dream of a "Wonderland" in which they have freedom and room to develop their feelings and wishes. But Berlin, which they thought would be their wonderland, turns a cold shoulder to the outsiders.

Dir.: Sandor Söth.
SP.: Sandor Söth, Geza Beremeny, Andras Mesz, Sandor Csukas.
Cam.: Andras Mesz, Sandor Csukas.
Mus.: Ferenc Darvas, Neurotic Group.
Prod.: Deutsche Film- und Fernsehakademie/Bela Balazs Filmstudio.
Act.: Laslo Kiss-Tamas, Beatrice Manowski, Tamas Pajor, Valeria Zsoldos, Birgit Anders.
80 min.

1988 *Der Philosoph (The Philosopher)*

Comedy in which a young, philosophical man meets three young women in contemporary Berlin who prove to be goddesses of love and introduce him to the Dionysian aspects of life.

Dir.: Rudolf Thome.
SP.: Rudolf Thome.
Cam.: Reinhold Vorschneider.
Mus.: Hanno Rinne.
Prod.: Moana-Film.
Act.: Johannes Herrschmann, Adriana Altaras, Friederike Tiefenbacher, Claudia Matschulla, Jürgen Wink.
83 min.

1987 *Plaza Real*

An architecht, living quietly in Spain, experiences a crisis of the soul when he meets a strange woman who resembles his wife exactly.

Dir.: Herbert Vesely.
SP.: Herbert Vesely.
Cam.: Rudolf Blahacek.
Mus.: Antonio Reyes, Francois Reyes, Patchai Reyes.
Prod.: Balance/Pro-ject/BR.
Act.: Jon Finch, Mia Nygren, Walter Buschhoff, Sonja Martin, José Maria Blanco.
99 min.

1985 *Der Polenweiher*

A young Polish woman, who had been brought to a farm in the Black Forest to be a worker in the last year of World War II, dies a mysterious death, which in turn sets off a chain of fateful political events.

>Dir.: Nico Hofmann.
>SP.: Thomas Strittmatter, Nico Hofmann.
>Cam.: Ernst J. Kubitza, Jan Kaiser.
>Mus.: Thomas Timmler, Dieter Gutfried.
>Prod.: Hofmann-Strittmatter Prod./SWR.
>Act.: Ursula Cantieni, Gerhard Olschewski, Wolf-Dietrich Sprenger, Eberhard Feik, Britta Pohland.
>104 min.

1986 *Punch Drunk*

As the Bavarian Secretary of State, Herbert Achternbusch deals with the sexual urges represented in his office, then is promoted to Minister of Culture, and finally ends up as a dead body floating in the water.

>Dir.: Herbert Achternbusch.
>SP.: Herbert Achternbusch.
>Cam.: Gunter Freyse, Herbert Achternbusch.
>Prod.: Herbert Achternbusch Filmprod.
>Act.: Herbert Achternbusch, Annamirl Bierbichler, Gabi Geist, Esther Donatz, Gunter Freyse.
>91 min.

1982 (German-Greek) *Pussycat Syndrome*

Two New York models vacation in Greece and experience a number of amorous adventures.

>Dir.: Ilia Milonako.
>SP.: Larry Dolgin.
>Mus.: Gerhard Heinz.

Prod.: Atlas Film & TV Prod./Andromeda International.
Act.: Jacqueline Marcan, Ajita Wilson, Herbert Hofer,
Tina Eklund, Cristus Nicoel.
90 min.

1987  *Der Radfahrer von San Christobal  (The Bicyclist from San Christobal)*

A young bicycle racer from Chile struggles to win the "Tour de Chile" so that, with the prize money, he can better care for his mother.

Dir.:   Peter Lilienthal.
SP.:    Antonio Skarmeta, Peter Lilienthal, from a story by Antonio Skarmeta.
Cam.:   Horst Yeidler.
Mus.:   Claus Bantzer.
Prod.:  Edgar Reitz Film/ZDF.
Act.:   René Baeza, Luz Jimenez, Roberto Navarrete, Dante Pesce, Javier Maldonado.
87 min.

1987  *Rage to kill*

The daughter of a Nazi hunter continues her mother's work after the latter is murdered, and discovers a concentration camp doctor in the jungles of Paraguay.

Dir.:   Ernst Ritter von Theumer.
SP.:    James Dallessandro, Louis La Russo II.
Cam.:   Mario Di Leo.
Mus.:   Larry Fallon.
Prod.:  TAT.
Act.:   Maud Adams, Stewart Granger, Candice Dali, Romulo Arantes, Wilhelm Berger.
99 min.

1984  (USA-German)  *Red Heat - Unschuld hinter Gittern  (Red Heat)*

121

A young American woman becomes a victim of the East German justice system.

Dir.:    Robert Collector.
SP.:     Robert Collector, Gary Drucker.
Cam.:    Wolfgang Dickmann.
Mus.:    Tangerine Dream.
Prod.:   Aida United/International Screen/T.A.T.
Act.:    Linda Blair, Sue Kiel, Sylvia Kristel, William Ostrander, Elisabeth Volkmann.
94 min.

1985-86  (German-Swiss)  *Die Reise  (The Journey)*

The factual story of generational conflict between a man (Will Vesper), who was a popular writer during the Nazi regime, and his son, who joined the radical student movement and, later, terrorist organizations.

Dir.:    Markus Imhoff.
SP.:     Markus Imhoff, from the novel by Bernward Vesper.
Cam.:    Hans Liechti.
Mus.:    Franco Ambrosetti.
Prod.:   Regina Ziegler/Liimbo/WDR/SRG.
Act.:    Markus Boysen, Corinna Kirchhoff, Claude Oliver Rudolph, Will Quadflieg, Alexander Mehner.
110 min.

1987  *Eine Reise nach Deutschland  (A Journey to Germany)*

A West German locksmith spontaneously accepts the invitation of an East German whom he barely knows to come visit in East Germany. There, he gets involved with a lovely seventeen-year-old, until her older sister, an officer in the People's Army, appears on the scene.

Dir.:    Heidi Genee.
SP.:     Jochen Ziem.
Cam.:    Hanning Zick.

Act.: Hannes Jaenicke, Nora Barner, Leo Bardischewski, Heike Faber, Christiane Carstens.

**1984** (German-Swiss) *Der Rekord (The World Record)*

Two small-time Munich video pirates attempt to set a new record - 240 hours of watching television - and thus gain new wealth.

Dir.: Daniel Helfer.
SP.: Daniel Helfer.
Cam.: Kay Gauditz.
Mus.: The Chance.
Prod.: HFFM/BR/Cactus Film/Schweizer Fernsehen.
Act.: Uwe Ochsenknecht, Laszlo I. Kish, Catarina Raake, Kurt Raab, Andras Fricsay.
85 min.

**1985** *Retouche*

After his father's death, a young man returns from Berlin to the small south German town of his youth, where he must decide whether to take over his father's camera store or sell it.

Dir.: Dieter Funk, Beat Lottaz.
SP.: Dieter Funk, Beat Lottaz.
Cam.: Peter van den Reek.
Mus.: Konrad Haas, Dominic Diaz.
Prod.: Deutsche Film- und Fernsehakademie Berlin.
Act.: Bernd Tauber, Gabi Pochert, Matina Gedeck, Marc Cevio, Barbara Boschan.
74 min.

**1985** *Richy Guitar*

After years of trying to get his big chance, a young man puts his own group together, but his troubles are just beginning.

Dir.: Michael Laux.
Cam.: Hans-Günther Bücking, Siegmar Brüggenthies.

Mus.:   Gazi Twist, Die Ärtze, Nena, Notorische Reflexe, Plan B.
Prod.:  Moviola GbR Dietmar Buchmann/Michael Laux.
Act.:   Jan Vetter, Dirk Felsenheimer, Hans Runge, Kristina Raschen, Ingrid van Bergen, Horst Pinnow.

90 min.

## 1988 (German-Swiss) *RobbyKallePaul*

Three friends who live in the same house and have all been disappointed in love decide to live without women.

Dir.:   Dani Levy.
SP.:    Dani Levy, Maria Schrader, Naja and Holger Franke.
Cam.:   Carl-Friedrich Koschnik.
Mus.:   Niki Reiser.
Prod.:  Luna/Fool/Levy/Koschnik/Atlas Saskia/Fama.
Act.:   Dani Levy, Frank Beilikke, Josef Hofmann, Anja Franke, Maria Schrader.
95 min.

## 1985 *Rosa Luxemburg*

The life and struggles of the socialist and pacifist Rosa Luxemburg.

Dir.:   Margarethe von Trotta.
SP.:    Margarethe von Trotta.
Cam.:   Franz Rath.
Mus.:   Nicolas Economou.
Prod.:  Bioskop/WDR.
Act.:   Barbara Sukowa, Hannes Jaenicke, Daniel Olbrychski, Doris Schade, Otto Sander.
123 min.

## 1988 *Rosalie Goes Shopping*

In an isolated town in Arkansas, Rosalie, the Bavarian wife of an

American G.I., uses every trick in the book to provide for her husband and children. Comedy.

Dir.: Percy Adlon.
SP.: Percy Adlon, Eleonore Adlon, Christopher Doherty.
Cam.: Bernd Heinl.
Mus.: Bob Telson.
Prod.: Pelemele.
Act.: Marianne Sägebrecht, Brad Davis, Judge Reinhold, Erika Blumberger, Willy Harlander.
94 min.

1989 *Rosamunde*

In Berlin in 1930, a young woman and three unemployed young men kidnap the son of wealthy Jews for ransom, but the woman falls in love with the son, and arguments abound between the kidnappers.

Dir.: Egon Günther.
SP.: Egon Günther.
Cam.: Gerard Vandenberg.
Mus.: Rolf Wilhelm.
Prod.: Mutoskop/Toro/Maran.
Act.: Anna Dobra, Jürgen Vogel, Richy Müller, Boris Koneczny, Mario Adorf.
111 min.

1989 (German-American) *Der Rosengarten (The Rose Garden)*

Following an attack on a former concentration camp commander, an old Jewish man in Frankfurt is taken to court. The man accepts this new suffering in order to bring to light the guilt of the man who was responsible for the deaths of twenty children.

Dir.: Fons Rademakers.
SP.: Paul Hengge, from his novel.
Cam.: Gernot Roll.
Mus.: Egisto Macchi.
Prod.: CCC Filmkunst/Cannon International.

Act.: Maximilian Schell, Liv Ullmann, Peter Fonda, Jan Niklas, Kurt Hübner.
112 min.

1984-86 (German-Portuguese) *Der Rosenkrieg (The Rose War)*

In an isolated area of Portugal, a woman and her grown son raise roses. His fanatical search for the perfect rose gradually melts with his fanatical love for a young thief whom he keeps prisoner.

Dir.: Werner Schroeter.
SP.: Werner Schroeter, Magdalena Montezuma.
Cam.: Elfi Mikesch.
Mus.: Verdi, Donizetti.
Prod.: Werner Schroeter Filmprod./Juliane-Lorenz-Filmprod./Futura.
Act.: Magdalena Montezuma, Mostefa Djadjam, Antonio Orlando.
106 min.

1985 (French-German) *Rote Küsse (Red Kisses)*

A young communist woman, who is an activist and the daughter of Polish emigrants, gets to know bourgeois life in Paris in 1952. When a friend returns from Russia and tells how badly things are going there, her perfect picture of a workers' paradise is destroyed.

Dir.: Vera Belmont.
SP.: Vera Belmont.
Cam.: Ramon Suarez.
Mus.: Jean-Marie Senia.
Prod.: Stephan Films/Films A 2/Farena Film/C & H Film.
Act.: Charlotte Valandrey, Lambert Wilson, Marthe Keller, Günter Lamprecht, Laurent Terzieff.
107 min.

1990 (German-Italian-French) *Die Rückkehr (The Return)*

A Parisian journalist has an affair with his wife's best friend, and the wife, a doctor, leaves for Africa. When she learns that her best friend is dying of cancer, she returns and, after long discussions, reconciles with both friend and husband.

Dir.: Margarethe von Trotta.
SP.: Margarethe von Trotta.
Cam.: Tonino Delli Colli.
Mus.: Eleni Karaindrou.
Prod.: Bioskop-Film/Scena Group/Rachel.
Act.: Barbara Sukowa, Stefania Sandrelli, Sami Frey, Jan Biczycki, Alexandere Mnouchkine.
105 min.

1985 (German-Italian) *Die Rückkehr der Wildgänse* *(The Return of the Wild Geese)*

Four frustrated veterans, who don't believe the official line that there are no American prisoners left in Vietnam, return there ten years after the war to see for themselves.

Dir.: Larry Ludman.
SP.: Gianfranco Clerici, Vincenzo Mannino, Fabrizio De Angelis, Erwin C. Dietrich.
Cam.: Sergio d'Offizi.
Mus.: Francesco de Masi.
Prod.: Ascot/Fulvia/VIP-Delta.
Act.: Christopher Connelly, Manfred Lehmann, John Steiner, Oliver Tobias, Donald Pleasance.
89 min.

1987  (German-Senegalese)  *Saaraba*

After living for seventeen years in Europe, a young African returns to his homeland of Senegal, only to find how much the people have adopted Western ways and given up their traditions.

Dir.:  Amadou Saalum Seck.
SP.:  Amadou Saalum Seck.
Cam.:  Thomas Merker.
Prod.:  HFFM/Azanie/Societe Nouvelle Promotion Cinematographique.
Act.:  Abdoul Azis Diop, Fabienne Joelle Felhio, Diankou Bakhayokho, Awa Cheickh Gueye, Elhdaj Abdoulaye Seck.
85 min.

1985-86  *Sarah*

After her husband's death, a wealthy Englishwoman living in Hamburg realizes that he left her in deep debt. She is first reduced to working as a high-class call girl, but soon finds herself in the seedy prostitution milieu of Hamburg.

Dir.:  Reginald Puhl.
SP.:  Jane Murray, Reginald Puhl.
Cam.:  Mike Marszalek, Dragan Rogulj.
Mus.:  Nya Murray, Andi Mason.
Prod.:  Reginald Puhl Filmprod.
Act.:  Jane Murray, Gunhild Branchart, Maria Schulenberg, Ralph Winkler, Monica Burrasch.
109 min.

1989  *Schatten der Wüste  (Shadow in the Desert)*

Two young Germans, who had been working as advisors at the edge
of the Sahara desert, get involved in an economic espionage affair,
and must escape through the desert, where their car breaks down.

Dir.:    Jürgen Bretzinger.
SP.:     Jürgen Bretzinger, Peter Renz.
Cam.:    Jürgen Jürges.
Mus.:    Andreas Köbner.
Prod.:   Voissfilm/Project/B.A. Prod./Neue Sentimental-
         Film/BR.
Act.:    Jessica Forde, Hannes Jaenicke, Oliver Stokowski,
         Joachim Kemmer, Adam Choucou.
99 min.

1990 (French-German) *Scheiß auf den Tod*

A young black man from the Antilles gets a job in a Paris nightclub
as "coach" for the cockfights. Just as he is beginning to reconsider his
relationship to his homeland, he is murdered.

Dir.:    Claire Denis.
SP.:     Jean-Pol Fargeau, Claire Denis.
Cam.:    Pascal Marti.
Mus.:    Abdullah Ibrahim.
Prod.:   Cinea/Pyramide/Les Films du Mindif/Camera
         One/NEF/La Sept.
Act.:    Isaach de Bankole, Alex Descas, Jean-Claude
         Brialy, Solveig Dommartin, Christopher Buchholz.
92 min.

1983 *Schimmi*

A young man who loses his apprenticeship gets together with some
friends to form a company that offers to get any job done fast.

Dir.:    Werner Masten.
SP.:     Jo Pestum, from his novel.
Cam.:    W.P. Hassenstein.
Prod.:   WDR.

Act.:    Sascha Disselkamp, Susanne Wolff, Mark
         Eichenseher, Marc Saint-Macavy, Sven Welper.
100 min.

1988 (German-Swiss) *Schlaflose Nächte (Sleepless Nights)*

Episodes from Berlin nightlife, in which young people search for
goals, happiness and love.

Dir.:    Marcel Gisler.
SP.:     Rudolf Nadler, Marcel Gisler.
Cam.:    Patrick Lindenmaier.
Prod.:   Valcano M/WDR/Kyros-Film/DRS.
Act.:    Rudolf Nadler, Anne Knaak, Cordula Stepanek,
         Andreas Herder, Matthias Tiefenbach.
99 min.

1987 *Schloß Königswald (Castle Königswald)*

Eight elderly ladies of nobility wait out the end of World War II in
a Bohemian castle, where they are alternately defended, protected
and freed by Germans, Americans and Russians. Finally, they flee
once more to their residence on the Rhine.

Dir.:    Peter Schamoni.
SP.:     Horst Bienek, Peter Schamoni, from a novel by
         Horst Bienek.
Cam.:    Gerard Vandenberg.
Mus.:    Ralf Siegel.
Prod.:   Peter Schamoni Prod./Allianz/ZDF.
Act.:    Camilla Horn, Carla Höhn, Marianne Hoppe, Fee
         von Reichlin, Marika Rökk.
89 min.

1986 *Schloß und Siegel (Lock and Seal)*

Comedy in which two prisoners develop a relationship as pen pals,
yet they are unsure whether they will still love each other when they
actually meet.

Dir.:    Heidi Ulmke.
SP.:     Geraldine Blecker, Heidi Ulmke.
Cam.:    Jörg Jeshel.
Mus.:    Peter W. Schmitt.
Prod.:   Frankfurter Filmwerkstatt/ZDF.
Act.:    Christiane Carstens, Karl Maslo, Susanne
         Bredehöft, Geraldine Blecker, Gerd Knebel.
81 min.

1987 *Schmetterlinge (Butterflies)*

Scenes from the life of a nineteen-year-old unemployed man who
lives in a shabby row house. One summer day, he is the only witness
to see a little girl from the neighborhood drown in an industrial
canal.

Dir.:    Wolfgang Becker.
SP.:     Wolfgang Becker, from a story by Ian McEwan.
Cam.:    Martin Kukula.
Prod.:   Deutsche Film- und Fernsehakademie (DFFB).
Act.:    Bertram von Boxberg, Lena Boehnicke, Dieter
         Oberholz, Uwe Helfrich, Peter Franke.
57 min.

1985 *Der Schneemann (The Snowman)*

Action comedy about a man who tries to make it big with five
kilograms of cocaine that he finds.

Dir.:    Peter F. Bringmann.
SP.:     Matthias Seelig, based on a novel by Jörg Fauser.
Cam.:    Helge Weindler.
Mus.:    Paul Vincent Gunia.
Prod.:   Bavaria/NF Geria II/ZDF.
Act.:    Marius Müller-Westernhagen, Polly Eltes, Heinz
         Wanitschek, Riad Gholmie, Manuela Riva.
100 min.

1985 *Die Schokoladen-Schnüffler (The Chocolate Sniffers)*

A Zurich detective solves mysterious murders from Zurich to London to Salzburg.

Dir.: Jiri Menzel
SP.: Erich Tomek, Sven Freiheit, from ideas by Edgar Wallace.
Cam.: Franz X. Lederle.
Prod.: Lisa/Roxy/K.S. Film/BR.
Act.: Rolf Knie, Gaston Häni, Susanne Uhlen, Werner Kreindl, Gert Burkhard.
89 min.

1988 *Schön war die Zeit (The Good Old Days)*

A film director, who had formerly worked for the official Nazi film production company, gets right back into making films after the war without showing any great remorse. Meanwhile, his cameraman friend suffers pangs of conscience about his past. Satire.

Dir.: Klaus Gietinger, Leo Hiemer.
SP.: Klaus Gietinger, Leo Hiemer, Marian Czura.
Cam.: Marian Czura.
Mus.: Klaus Roggors.
Prod.: Westallgäuer Filmprod./Maran/B.A.
Act.: Gottfried John, Edgar Selge, Ewa Blaszczyk, Joachim Bernhard, Jessica Kosmalla.
115 min.

1989 *Der Schönste (Handsome)*

"Der Schönste" is the nickname of a Frankfurt vagrant with money, ambition and plans for the future, who gets into trouble when he loses his money.

Dir.: Burghard Schlicht.
SP.: Burghard Schlicht.
Cam.: Jörg Jeshel.

Mus.:  Rio Reiser.
Prod.:  Daniel Zuta-Burghard Schlicht Filmprod./ZDF.
Act.:  Burghard Schlicht, Ling Tai, Rolf Idler, Rio Reiser,
        Circe.
90 min.

1990  *Das schreckliche Mädchen (The Nasty Girl)*

Sonja, a young schoolgirl, conducts research for an essay contest on
the theme "My Home Town during the Third Reich," and is
confronted with resistance, mistrust and suspicion.

Dir.:  Michael Verhoeven.
SP.:  Michael Verhoeven.
Cam.:  Axel de Roche.
Mus.:  Mike Herting, Elmar Schloter, Billy Gorlt, Lydie
        Auvray.
Prod.:  Sentana/ZDF.
Act.:  Lena Stolze, Monika Baumgartner, Michael Gahr,
        Hans-Reinhard Müller, Robert Giggenbach.
92 min.

1985  *Schulmädchen - Reif für die Liebe (School Girls - Ready for Love)*

A would-be director who needs money for his next project decides to
use a wealthy high school girl to get it.

Dir.:  Ilia Milonako.
SP.:  Vagelis Fournistakis.
Mus.:  Giovanni Ullu.
Prod.:  Atlas International.
Act.:  Marcella Petri, Roger Beach, Mario Cutini, Teli
        Stalone, Pauline Teutscher.
79 min.

1985  *Schwabinger Girls*

A young woman loses her job because she is not interested in sexual escapades, then starts running with the Schwabing crowd in Munich, where she gets entangled in such escapades anyway.

Dir.:   Jörg Michael.
Cam.:   Günter Lemmer.
Mus.:   Basement Child Band.
Prod.:   Hardy Wagner.
Act.:   Michaela Schindler, Corinna Jansen, Hans Peter Gillich, Heidrun Krenner.
78 min.

1985 *Schwarz und ohne Zucker (Black and without Sugar)*

During a vacation in Italy a young German man falls in love with an Icelandic movie star.

Dir.:   Lutz Konermann.
SP.:   Lutz Konermann.
Cam.:   Tom Fährmann.
Mus.:   Egill Olafson, Adrian Vonwiller.
Prod.:   Optische Werke/Salinas/BR/NDR.
Act.:   Lutz Konermann, Edda Heidrun Backmann, Gudjon Pedersen, Kolbrun Halldorsdottir, Hanna Maria Karlsdottir.
85 min.

1986 (Swiss-Austrian-German) *Der schwarze Tanner (The Black Forester)*

A Swiss miner refuses to the end to obey a law that appears to him to be illogical and destructive.

Dir.:   Xavier Koller.
SP.:   Xavier Koller, Walter Deuber, from a story by Meinrad Inglin.
Cam.:   Elemer Ragalyi.
Mus.:   Hardy Hepp.
Prod.:   Catpics/SRG/ZDF/ORF/Egli/Glass.
Act.:   Otto Mächtlinger, Renate Steiger, Liliana

Heimberg, Susanne Betschart, Elisabeth Seiler.
107 min.

1985 *Schwarzer Lohn und weisse Weste (The White-Collar Black Economy)*

Herbert König deals in the "black economy" of illegal employment, moonlighting, etc., until he is rounded up by a new government agency.

Dir.: Marco Serafini.
Cam.: Lothar Stickelbrucks.
Prod.: Horizont Filmprod.
Act.: Peer Schmidt, Raphael Wilcek, Hagen Mueller-Stahl, Karl-Walter Diess, Klaus Münster, Manfred Lehmann, Katharina Graefe, Brigitte Mira.
70 min.

1986 *Das Schweigen des Dichters (The Writer's Silence)*

An Israeli writer has stopped writing because he no longer believes in the healing power of the written word. But when his son, who is mentally retarded, learns the value of language, the man is challenged to rethink his beliefs.

Dir.: Peter Lilienthal.
SP.: Peter Lilienthal, from a story by Abraham B. Jehoschua.
Cam.: Justus Pankau.
Mus.: Claus Bantzer.
Prod.: Edgar Reitz Film/WDR.
Act.: Jakov Lind, Len Ramras, Daniel Dedem, Towje Kleiner, Vladimir Weigel.
102 min.

1988-89 *Schweinegeld - Ein Märchen der Gebrüder Nimm* (C*A*S*H - A Political Fairy Tale)

Comedy in which three smalltime crooks try to foil the attempts of corrupt politicians to smuggle weapons illegally.

Dir.: Norbert Kückelmann.
SP.: Norbert Kückelmann, Michael Juncker, Dagmar Kekule.
Cam.: Frank Brühne.
Mus.: Hanno Rinne, Gabriele di Rosa.
Prod.: FFAT/Maran-Film/Pro-ject/Kairos Film.
Act.: Armin Mueller-Stahl, Claudia Messner, Rolf Zacher, Stefan Suske, Hans-Michael Rehberg.
91 min.

1988 (German-Swiss) *Ein Schweizer namens Nötzli (A Swiss Named Nötzli)*

Through an error, a bookkeeper in a chemicals company ends up in the boss's seat, whence he directs the company's activities to everyone's satisfaction. When the "real" boss shows up, Nötzli is demoted again.

Dir.: Gustav Ehmck.
SP.: Ralph Engler, Walter Roderer, from ideas from a play by Hans Schubert.
Cam.: Peter Baumgartner.
Mus.: Walter Baumgartner.
Prod.: Ascot-Film/Dietrich-Burger-Roderer.
Act.: Walter Roderer, Jochen Schroeder, Ursela Monn, Julia Biedermann, Ruth Jecklin.
103 min.

1988 *Der Senkrechtstarter*

Futuristic movie that takes place in the year 1999, in which two men must help a woman get free of her tedious job returning merchandise to a "central bank."

Dir.: Christian Rateuke.
SP.: Christian Rateuke, Christoph Treutwein.
Cam.: Atze Glanert.

Mus.:   Jürgen Knieper.
Prod.:  Ufa Filmprod.
Act.:   Mike Krüger, Christina Plate, Karl Dall, Andras
        Fricsay, Kali Son.
88 min.

1985  *Der sexte Sinn (The Sexth Sense)*

Two brothers who have grown up under the strong influence of their
mother fall in love with the same woman.

Dir/SP: Dagmar Beiersdorf, Lothar Lambert.
Cam.:   Hans Günter Bücking.
Mus.:   Albert Kittler.
Prod.:  Horizont Filmprod.
Act.:   Albert Heins, Ingolf Gorges, Ulrike Schirm, Ela
        Behrends, Barbara Morawiecz, Jutta Klöppel,
        Susanne Stahl.

1989  *Sieben Frauen  (Seven Women)*

A modern fairy tale in which Hans, the prodigal son, returns to
inherit his father's estate and is confronted with millions of marks,
dubious business dealings, and five daughters who want to marry him.

Dir.:   Rudolf Thome.
SP.:    Rudolf Thome.
Cam.:   Martin Gressmann.
Mus.:   Wolfgang Böhmer.
Prod.:  Moana-Film.
Act.:   Johannes Herrschmann, Adriana Altaras, Elisabeth
        Zündel, Alexandra Schnaubelt, Margarete Raspe.
89 min.

1986  *Sierra Leone*

After working three years as a truck driver in the West African Bush,
a man returns to the Federal Republic of Germany, where he has
difficulties finding a niche for himself.  He begins to travel the land

without any particular goal, hoping to realize his dream of a free life.

Dir.: Uwe Schrader.
SP.: Klaus Müller-Laue, Uwe Schrader.
Cam.: Klaus Müller-Laue.
Mus.: Bülent Ersoy, Garnet Gimms & The Enchanters.
Prod.: Uwe Schrader Filmprod./BR.
Act.: Christian Redl, Ann Gisel Glass, Rita Russek, Constanze Engelbracht, Andras Fricsay, Kali Son.
92 min.

1988 *Singles*

A young man, whose lover has left him, has a difficult time adjusting to the singles life, and his self-pity begins to affect his professional as well as private life.

Dir.: Ecki Ziedrich.
SP.: Ecki Ziedrich.
Cam.: Egon Werdin.
Mus.: Lothar Krell, Thomas Lohr.
Prod.: Frankfurter Filmwerkstatt.
Act.: Helmut Zierl, Leonard Lansink, Claudia Demarmels, Nina Hoger, Jan Fedder.
80 min.

1990 (German-French) *Sissi - der Film (Sissi - The Movie)*

The somewhat mysterious circumstances surrounding the succession of Sissi to the Austrian throne.

Dir.: Christoph Böll.
SP.: Christoph Böll.
Cam.: Reinhard Köcher.
Prod.: Calypso Film/Uwe Franke/Werner Possardt/Köln Maran Film/Stuttgart/New Deal Film/Paris.
Act.: Vanessa Wagner, Nils Tavernier, Sonja Kirchberger, Jean Poiret, Kristina Walter, Cleo Kretschmer.
90 min.

1989  *Der Skipper  (The Skipper)*

On board a yacht, the tension and jealousy between the skipper and
his two young women passengers become so great that they end in
death.

Dir.:    Peter Keglevic.
SP.:     Peter Keglevic.
Cam.:    Edward Klosinski.
Mus.:    Brynmor Jones.
Prod.:   Rialto Film/WDR.
Act.:    Jürgen Prochnow, Patsy Kensit, Elizabeth Hurley,
         Franz Buchrieser, Grazyna Szapolowska.
98 min.

1986  (German-U.S.)  *Sleepwalk*

A young woman unwittingly gets involved in the seamy side of New
York nightlife.

Dir.:    Sara Driver.
SP.:     Sara Driver, Lorenzo Mans.
Cam.:    Jim Jarmusch.
Mus.:    Phil Kline.
Prod.:   Ottoskop/Driver.
Act.:    Suzanne Fletcher, Ann Magnuson, Dexter Lee,
         Steven Chen, Tony Todd.
80 min.

1987  *Der Sommer des Falken  (The Summer of the Falcon)*

A shy, timid boy from the big city meets up with a farm girl in the
mountains of southern Tyrolia.  Together, they help capture a man
who has been stealing falcon eggs from their nests and selling them
to Arabs.

Dir.:    Arend Agthe.
SP.:     Arend Agthe, Monika Seck-Agthe.
Cam.:    Jürgen Jürges.

Mus.: Matthias Raue, Martin Cyrus.
Prod.: Topas/Atlas Saskia/WDR.
Act.: Andrea Lösch, Janos Crecelius, Rolf Zacher, Hermann Lause, Volker Brandt.
106 min.

1985 *Der Sommer des Samurai* (*The Summer of the Samurai*)

A Hamburg businessman, who believes strongly in Japanese traditions, avenges the theft of a Samurai sword.

Dir.: Hans-Christoph Blumenberg.
SP.: Hans-Christoph Blumenberg, Carola H. Stern, Frederik Spindale.
Cam.: Wolfgang Dickmann.
Mus.: Hubert Bartholomae.
Prod.: Radiant.
Act.: Cornelia Froboess, Hans Peter Hallwachs, Wojtek Pszoniak, Nadja Tiller, Peter Kraus.
104 min.

1987 (German-Italian) *Space Pirates*

Loosely based on "Treasure Island," this movie has the treasure located in outer space, and the pirate adventures take place as a space odyssey.

Dir.: Antonio Margheriti.
SP.: Renato Castellani, Lucio de Caro, from a novel by Robert L. Stevenson.
Cam.: Sandro Messina.
Mus.: Gianfranco Plenizio.
Prod.: Bavaria/RAI/Canale S/TF 1.
Act.: Anthony Quinn, Itaco Nardulli, Philippe Leroy, Klaus Löwitsch, Ulrich von Dobschütz.
114 min.

1971 (Italian-German-Yugoslavian) *Spezialkommando Wildgänse* (*Special Command Force Wild Geese*)

The British military unit on Cyprus battles against an underground organization led by a rebellious priest.

Dir.: Robert McCahon (=Adriano Bolzoni).
SP.: Finley Hunt (=Brosi Mihailovic), Alan White (=Gunther Heller), Robert McCahon (=Adriano Bolzini), from a novel by William H. Gage, Jr.
Cam.: Guglielmo Garroni.
Mus.: Gianni Ferrio.
Prod.: Roberto Cinematografica/Lisa/Avala Genex.
Act.: Michael Craig, Eva Renzi, Klaus Kinski, Adolfo Celi, George Sanders.
93 min.

1989 *Spieler (Gamblers)*

A good-for-nothing young gambling addict falls in love with his cousin and tries to combine his passion for the woman with his passion for gambling.

Dir.: Dominik Graf.
SP.: Christoph Fromm, Dominik Graf.
Cam.: Klaus Eichhammer.
Mus.: Andreas Köhner, Dominik Graf.
Prod.: Bavaria/ZDF.
Act.: Peter Lohmeyer, Anica Dobra, Hansa Czypionka, Joachim Kammer, Anthony Dawson.
111 min.

1983 (German-French) *Die Spieler (The Gamblers)*

A man obsessed with gambling goes through life dreaming of the "big win" and dragging others down with him.

Dir.: Barbet Schroeder.
SP.: Barbet Schroeder, Pascal Bonitzer, Steve Baes, from a novel by Steve Baes.
Cam.: Robby Mueller.
Mus.: Peer Raben.

Prod.: Bioskop/B.A. Prod./Les Films du Losange/FR
3/Metro Filme/NEF.
Act.: Jacques Dutronc, Bulle Ogier, Kurt Raab, Virgilio
Teixeira, Steve Baes.
95 min.

## 1986-88 *Das Spinnennetz (The Spider's Web)*

Movie of Joseph Roth's first novel, in which a former lieutenant
begins to put his world back together after the defeat in 1918. He
gets involved in an extreme right-wing organization, and no task is
too cruel or bloody when it comes to climbing the career ladder.

Dir.: Bernhard Wicki.
SP.: Wolfgang Kirchner, Bernhard Wicki, from a novel
by Joseph Roth.
Cam.: Gerard Vandenberg.
Mus.: Günther Fischer.
Prod.: Provobis/ZDF/Beta-Film/ORF/RAI-2/TVE/Film-
export Bratislava.
Act.: Ulrich Mühe, Klaus Maria Brandauer, Armin
Mueller-Stahl, Andrea Jonasson, Corinna Kirchhoff.
196 min.

## 1984 *Sprit für Spatzen (Gas for the Kids)*

When a twelve-year-old boy dies from an alcohol overdose, parents
and educators try to prevent the same fate in other children.

Dir.: Günter Hoffmann.
SP.: Günter Hoffmann.
Cam.: Horst Schönberger.
Mus.: H. Pagel, Gert Wilden.
Prod.: Melophon-Film/Kuratorium junger deutscher Film.
Act.: Erik Schumann, Kerstin de Ahna, Philipp Brammer,
Claudia Uttler, Michael Gahr.
90 min.

1985  *Die Stadtpiraten  (The City Pirates)*

The Berlin children's gang "City Pirates" gets hold of a suitcase belonging to the American military, and thus they get involved in a tremendous adventure with an American special agent.

> Dir.:    Rolf Silber.
> SP.:     Rolf Silber.
> Cam.:    Wolfram Seibt.
> Mus.:    Peter W. Schmidt.
> Prod.:   Frankfurter Filmwerkstatt/Sender Freies Berlin.
> Act.:    Ron Williams, Philip Spohn, Julia Martinek, Roy Scholz, Thomas Nowald.
> 61 min.

1985  *Stammheim*

Story of the 192-day trial of the Baader-Meinhof Gang, also known as the Red Army Faction terrorist organization.

> Dir.:    Reinhard Hauff.
> SP.:     Stefan Aust.
> Cam.:    Frank Brühne, Günter Wulff.
> Mus.:    Marcel Wengler.
> Prod.:   Bioskop/Thalia-Theater.
> Act.:    Ulrich Pleitgen, Ulrich Tukur, Therese Affolter, Sabine Wegner, Hans Kremer.
> 107 min.

1987-88  *Starke Zeiten  (Crazy Times)*

Six episodes featuring popular movie and TV stars.

> Dir.:    Siggi Götz, Klaudi Fröhlich, Rolf Olsen, Otto W. Retzer.
> Cam.:    Heinz Hoelscher, Franz X. Lederle.
> Prod.:   K.S./Lisa/Roxy.
> Act.:    Helmut Fischer, Hans-Joachim Kulenkampff, Otto Schenk, Hias, Zachi Noy.

92 min.

1986 (German-Sri Lankan) *Der Stein des Todes* (*The Stone of Death*)

A man whose lover has fallen victim to the drug dealers of Sri Lanka seeks revenge.

Dir.: Franz Josef Gottlieb.
SP.: Heinz Werner John, Werner Hauff.
Cam.: Klaus Werner.
Prod.: Neue Regina-film/CCC Filmkunst/BR/Taprobane.
Act.: Heather Thomas, Albert Fortell, Siegfried Rauch, Elke Sommer, Christian Anders.
97 min.

1989 (German-Swiss) *Stille Betrüger* (*Sleepy Betrayers*)

Paul attempts to break up with Sandra without "hurting" her; his friend Georg helps for his own reasons.

Dir.: Beat Lottaz.
SP.: Beat Lottaz, Jörg Helbling.
Cam.: Rainer Meissle.
Mus.: Marius Odagiu.
Prod.: DFFB, Imago Z, Jörg Helbling, Zürich.
Act.: Muzzu Muzzulini/Annemarie Knaak/Andreas Schmidt/Elke Reichardt/Jale Arikan/Bernd Ludwig.
84 min.

1989 (German-French-Italian) *Stille Tage in Clichy* (*Quiet Days in Clichy*)

An elderly man recounts for a young girl his days in Paris in the 30s and how he and his friend bounced from one sexual adventure to the next.

Dir.: Claude Chabrol.

SP.:    Ugo Lenzio, Claude Chabrol, from a novel by
        Henry Miller.
Cam.:   Jean Rabier.
Mus.:   Matthieu Chabrol, Luigi Ceccarelli, Jena-Michel
        Bernard.
Prod.:  Direkt/Intalfrance/AZ.
Act.:   Andrew McCarthy, Nigel Havers, Barbara de Rossi,
        Stephanie Cotta, Isolde Barth.
121 min.

1988 *Die Stimme* (*The Voice*)

A group of people are held prisoner and terrorized in a floating
discotheque overnight.

Dir.:   Gustavo Graef-Marino.
SP.:    Gustavo Graef-Marino.
Cam.:   Egon Werdin.
Mus.:   Jens-Peter Ostendorf.
Prod.:  Radiant/Salinas.
Act.:   Jon Finch, Suzanna Hamilton, Uwe Ochsenknecht,
        Heinz Hoenig, Richy Müller.
90 min.

1985 *Strawberry Fields*

Charlotte and Karl, on a trip across Germany, try to convert others
to their new political movement, which mixes environmental concerns
with right-wing ideology.

Dir.:   Kristian Kühn.
SP.:    Kristian Kühn, Stephan Poliakoff.
Cam.:   Martin Schäfer.
Prod.:  Marten Taege Filmprod./Channel 4.
Act.:   Beate Jensen, Rolf Zacher, Thomas Schmücke, Lisa
        Kreuzer, Wolfgang Wahl, Iris Disse, Dieter Traier.
82 min.

1988-89 *Sturzflug* (*Nose Dive*)

Two harbor workers from Lübeck change their romanticized views about the South Seas when they win a large sum of money gambling and take a trip to Thailand.

Dir.:   Thorsten Näter.
SP.:    Thorsten Näter.
Cam.:   Thorsten Näter, Wolfgang Becker.
Mus.:   Alexander Traut.
Prod.:  Thorsten Näter Filmproduktion/ZDF.
Act.:   Wilfried Dziallas, Wolfgang Finck, Brigitta Dresewski, Gesa Badenhorst, Horst Lütkens.
105 min.

1988 *Sukkubus*

On an isolated mountain, two men and a young boy build a woman out of roots and rags; she comes to life and destroys them, because she is the devil herself.

Dir.:   Georg Tressler.
SP.:    Franz Seitz.
Cam.:   Rudolf Blahacek.
Mus.:   Rudolf Wilhelm.
Prod.:  Franz Seitz Filmprod./Roxy.
Act.:   Peter Simonischek, Giovanni Früh, Andy Voß, Pamely Prati.
80 min.

1985  (German-Swiss)  *Tagediebe  (Day Thieves)*

Scenes from the lives of two young men and a young woman who live together in an old building in Berlin, support themselves with odd jobs, and try not to get discouraged.

     Dir.:    Marcel Gisler.
     SP.:     Marcel Gisler.
     Cam.:   Rüdiger Weiss, Prsica Forter.
     Mus.:   Various, chosen by Marcel Gisler.
     Prod.:  Marcel Gisler Filmprod./Renz Film (for ZDF).
     Act.:    Rudolf Nadler, Dina Leipzig, Lutz Deisinger, Matheiu Hornung.
     100 min.

1986  *Tarot*

An actress and a film director retreat to a house in the country to discuss their relationship. Problems arise when the man's friend and the woman's niece are invited to join them.

     Dir.:    Rudolf Thome.
     SP.:     Max Zihlmann, on themes from Goethe's "Elective Affinities."
     Cam.:   Martin Schäfer.
     Mus.:   Christoph Oliver.
     Prod.:  Moana/Athea/ZEF.
     Act.:    Vera Tschechowa, Hanns Zischler, Rüdiger Vogler, Katharina Böhm, William Berger.
     120 min.

1985  *Der Tausch  (The Exchange)*

A "Schimanski" story, involving terrorists; from the "Tatort" series.

> Dir.: Ilse Hofmann.
> SP.: Chiem van Houweninge, Hartmut Grund.
> Cam.: Kalr Kases.
> Mus.: Dieter Bohlen.
> Prod.: Bavaria/WDR.
> Act.: Götz George, Eberhard Feik, Ulrich Matschoss, Yolane Gilot, Nicole Ansari.
> 90 min.

1987 *Taxi nach Kairo* (*Taxi to Cairo*)

A homosexual man could inherit lots of money and a large farm if he would marry. He thus engages in a fictitious marriage, but develops a lasting, strong friendship with the woman.

> Dir.: Frank Ripploh.
> SP.: Tamara Kafka, Frank Ripploh.
> Cam.: Dodo Simonic.
> Mus.: Peter Breiner.
> Prod.: Frank Ripploh.
> Act.: Frank Ripploh, Christina Neubauer, Udo Schnek, Nina Schühly, Domenica Niehoff.
> 90 min.

1986 (French-German-Hungarian) *Terminus*

In the year 2037, the world is divided into two camps. Scientists want to support a government of militant barbarians and are cloning people to create many beings to fight their battles. A young boy clone, however, develops a mind of his own and foils their plans.

> Dir.: Pierre-William Glenn.
> SP.: Pierre William Glenn, Patrice Davic.
> Cam.: Jean-Claude Vicquery.
> Mus.: David Cunningham.
> Prod.: CART/Les Films du Cheval de FER/Initial Groupe CBL Films/Films A2.

Act.:    Johnny Hallyday, Karen Allen, Jürgen Prochnow,
         Gabriel Daman, Julie Glenn.
81 min.

1987  (English-German)  *The Dead - Die Toten  (The Dead)*

Following the traditional family get-together on Epiphany, a man
realizes what an insubstantial role he has played in his wife's life.
Based on James Joyce.

Dir.:    John Huston.
SP.:     John Huston, based on a story by James Joyce.
Cam.:    Fred Murphy.
Mus.:    Alex North.
Prod.:   Zenith Prod.
Act.:    Anjelica Huston, Donald McCann, Helena Caroll,
         Cathleen Delany, Ingrid Craigie.
83 min.

1988  *Tiger, Löwe, Panther  (Tiger, Lion, Panther)*

Three women of various temperaments attempt to break out of their
daily routine and support one another through their friendship.

Dir.:    Dominik Graf.
SP.:     Sherry Hormann.
Cam.:    Klaus Eichhammer.
Mus.:    Andreas Koebner, Dominik Graf.
Prod.:   Bavaria Film.
Act.:    Natja Bruckhorst, Martina Gedeck, Sabine Kaack,
         Thomas Winkler, Oliver Stokowski.
97 min.

1986  (German-French)  *Der Tod des Empedokles  (Empedocles'
Death)*

Scenes of the life and voluntary death of the Greek philosopher
Empedocles, based on fragments by Hölderlin.

Dir.: Jean-Marie Straub, Daniele Huillet.
SP.: Jean-Marie Straub, Daniele Huillet, from a fragment of a tragedy by Friedrich Hölderlin.
Cam.: Renato Berta, Jean Paul Toraille, Giovanni Canfarelli.
Prod.: Janus/Les Films du Losange.
Act.: Andreas von Rauch, Howard Vernon, Vladimir Baratta, Martina Baratta, Ute Cremer.
132 min.

1985  *Der Tod des weißen Pferdes (Death of a White Horse)*

The strained relationship between a monastery and the surrounding village at the time of the Peasant Wars of the early sixteenth century.

Dir/SP: Christian Ziewer.
Cam.: Gerard Vandenberg.
Mus.: Erhard Grosskopf.
Prod.: Basis/WDR.
Act.: Thomas Anzenhofer, Angela Schanelec, Udo Samel, Peter Franke, Dietmar Schönherr.
110 min.

1985  (USA-German)  *Tod eines Handlungsreisenden  (Death of a Salesman)*

Film of Arthur Miller's famous play, adapted by Volker Schlöndorff.

Dir.: Volker Schlöndorff.
SP.: Arthur Miller, from his play.
Cam.: Michael Ballhaus.
Mus.: Alex North.
Prod.: Roxbury/Punch/Bioskop.
Act.: Dustin Hoffman, Kate Reid, John Malkovich, Stephen Lang, Charles Durning.
134 min.

1978-79 (Brazilian-German) *Die Todesbrigade (The Death Brigade)*

An armored vehicle carrying money is brutally attacked and all the guards are killed.

Dir.:     Fauzi Mansur.
SP.:      Fauzi Mansur.
Cam.:     Claudio Portiolli.
Prod.:    J. Davila Prod./Onyx-Film.
Act.:     Vera Fischer, Roberto Bolant, David Cardoso, Marlene Franca.
77 min.

### 1986 *Tommaso Blu*

A southern Italian factory worker, who is frustrated by his work and his marriage, seeks refuge in nature and searches for love and human compassion.

Dir.:     Florian Furtwängler.
SP.:      Tommaso Di Ciaula, Peter Kammerer, Florian Furtwängler, from a novel by Tommaso Di Ciaula.
Cam.:     James Jacobs.
Mus.:     Peer Raben.
Prod.:    Florian Furtwängler/BR.
Act.:     Alessandro Haber, lay actors.
90 min.

### 1986 *Total bescheuert (Totally Crazy)*

Comedy in which three less than intellectual brothers are promised a great deal of inheritance money if they complete three difficult tasks.

Dir.:     Harald Alexander.
SP.:      Werner Krumbiegel, Harald Alexander.
Cam.:     Martin Abert, Thomas Abert.
Mus.:     Kunterbunt, Grenzwacht Stabil.
Prod.:    Silvia.
Act.:     Heinrich Hambitzer, Linda Relton, Victor Brown, Herbert Meurer, Ralph Willman.

90 min.

1985-86  *Transittäume  (Transitional Dreams)*

Two women, one from West Berlin, one from East Berlin, exchange property, apartments, clothing and husbands, not to mention professions, and encounter many problems.

Dir.:   Hartmut Jahn.
SP.:    Hartmut Jahn, Peter Wensierski.
Cam.:   Carlos Bustamante.
Mus.:   Bernhard Voss.
Prod.:  panta/ZDF.
Act.:   Marita Marschall, Pascal Lavy, Gerald Uhlig, Edith Neitzel, Kurt Raab.
95 min.

1986  *Ein Treffen mit Rimbaud  (A Meeting with Rimbaud)*

A young female hitchhiker is picked up by a middle-aged gangster, and he takes her along with him to the South.  On the way, she learns of his mysterious past, and the trip ends in disaster.

Dir.:   Ernst-August Zurborn.
SP.:    Ernst-August Zurborn.
Cam.:   Thomas Mauch.
Mus.:   Brynmor Jones.
Prod.:  Panorama/Pro-ject/BR.
Act.:   Anke Sevenich, Sven Wollter, Hannelore Elsner, Klaus Behrend, Walter Kreye.
87 min.

1987  *Das Treibhaus  (The Greenhouse)*

Movie version of Wolfgang Koeppen's 1953 novel, which takes a stand on German re-armament, the division of Germany and political morality.

Dir.:   Peter Goedel.

SP.: Peter Goedel, from the novel by Wolfgang Koeppen.
Cam.: David Slama.
Mus.: Richard Wagner.
Prod.: Peter Goedel Filmprod./WDR/BR/HR/NDR/ SWF/cult film tv.
Act.: Christian Doermer, Laila Florentine Freer, Jörg Hube, Hanns Zischler, Rüdiger Vogler (narrator).
99 min.

1987 (German-Czech-Austrian) *Der treue Johannes (Loyal Johann)*

Film version of the Grimm fairy tale, in which the servant, Johann, has promised to stand by his master, the prince, until the latter has matured into a man. When the prince decides to rescue the "Golden Virgin" from the evil Lord of the Gold, Johannes must protect the couple from all danger.

Dir.: Slavo Luther.
SP.: Slavo Luther, Martin Porubjak, from ideas from a fairy tale from the Grimm brothers.
Prod.: Omnia/Slovenska filmova tvorba/ZDF/ORF.
Act.: Vladimir Hajdu, Remi Martin, Maru Valdivielso, Heinz Moog, Lara Naszinski.
94 min.

1985-86 *Triumph der Gerechten (Triumph of the Just)*

Scenes shift from the Bavaria of the seventeenth century to present-day carnival parades, threatening speeches by intellectuals and clergymen, etc., until an atomic bomb explodes and catapults humanity back to its beginnings.

Dir.: Josef Bierbichler.
SP.: Josef Bierbichler, from a story by Oskar Maria Graf.
Cam.: Jörg Schmidt-Reitwein.
Mus.: Rudolf Gregor Knabl, Ludwig van Beethoven.
Prod.: Bierbichler-Filmprod.

Act.:    Josef Bierbichler, Rudi Klaffenböck, Alfons Scharf,
         Annemarie Bierbichler, Edgar Liegl.
81 min.

1984  *Tunguska - Die Kisten sind da  (Tunguska - The Cartons are*
**Here)**

Experimental film that combines elements of adventure, science
fiction, horror and romance.

Dir.:    Christoph Schlingensief.
SP.:     Christoph Schlingensief.
Cam.:    Dominikus Probst.
Mus.:    Christoph Schlingensief, Baba Zoro Diob, Christoph
         Gerozissis, Mathias Colli.
Prod.:   Schlingensief.
Act.:    Irene Fischer, Mathias Colli, Anna Fechter,
         Christopher Krieg, Alfred Edel.
75 min.

1989  *Überall ist es besser, wo wir nicht sind  (The Grass is Greener Everywhere Else)*

A young Polish man from Warsaw gets stranded in West Berlin on his way to fulfilling his dreams in America.

>
> Dir.:   Michael Klier.
> SP.:   Michael Klier.
> Cam.:   Sophie Maintigneux.
> Prod.:   Daniel Zuta Filmprod./ZDF.
> Act.:   Miroslaw Baka, Marta Klubowicz, Michael Krause, Josef Zebrowski, Anna Pastewka.
> 74 min.

1989  *Überleben in New York  (Survival in New York)*

The movie describes the destinies of three German women who broke out of their German norm and have been living in New York through thick and thin for ten years.

>
> Dir.:   Rosa von Praunheim.
> SP.:   Rosa von Praunheim.
> Cam.:   Jeff Preiss.
> Mus.:   Roy Campbell.
> Prod.:   Rosa von Praunheim/WDR.
> Act.:   Claudia, Anna, Uli.
> 90  min.

1985  *Der Unbesiegbare (The Invincible)*

Three earthlings travel to Mars to protect the earth from the evil Argon, and their adventures appear on earth as a TV series.

Dir/SP: Gusztav Hamos.
Cam.:   Wolfgang Knigge.
Mus.:   Martin Daske.
Prod.:  Salinas Film/ZDF.
Act.:   Kurt von Ruffin, Heinz Kammer, Hans-Peter
        Hallwachs, Mike A. Hentz, Lotti Huber, Udo Kier.
85 min.

1989 (German-French-Italian) *Und es ward Licht* *(And There Was Light)*

Life in an African village with a matriarchal society is virtually destroyed by the invasion of "civilization."

Dir.:   Otar Iosseliani.
SP.:    Otar Iosseliani.
Cam.:   Robert Alazraki.
Mus.:   Nicolas Zourabichvili.
Prod.:  Direkt Film/Les Films du Triangle/La Sept/RAI
        Uno.
Act.:   Saly Badji, Binta Cisse, Sigalon Sagna, Moussa
        Sagna, Oswaldo Olivera.
106 min.

1989 *Die unendliche Geschichte II - Auf der Suche nach Phantasien (The Neverending Story II)*

Young Bastian travels again to the land of Fantasia in order to save the land from an evil wizard.

Dir.:   George Miller.
SP.:    Karin Howard, from ideas from a novel by Michael
        Ende.
Cam.:   David Connell.
Mus.:   Robert Folk.
Prod.:  The Neverending Story Film/Cine Vox.
Act.:   Jonathan Brandis, Kenny Morrison, Clarissa Burt,
        Alexandra Johns, Martin Umbach.
90 min.

## 1985  *Unser Mann im Dschungel  (Jungle Mission)*

A German engineer, who is overseeing the construction of a dam in Equador, crashes in a plane in the middle of the jungle.

Dir.: Rudolf Steiner, Peter Stripp.
SP.: Peter Stripp.
Cam.: Helge Weindler.
Mus.: Manfred Hübler.
Prod.: Provobis/SWF.
Act.: Armin Mueller-Stahl, Katja Rupe, Simen Rühaak, Samuel Caento Padilla, Edica Grefa.
101 min.

## 1986-87  *Der Unsichtbare  (The Invisible)*

Comedy in which a TV moderator comes into possession of a magic hood that makes him invisible and enables him to learn of his wife's infidelity.

Dir.: Ulf Miehe.
SP.: Ulf Miehe, Klaus Richter.
Cam.: Frany Rath.
Mus.: Boris Jojic.
Prod.: Luna/Solaris/Neue  Constantin/Heidi  Genee Filmprod.
Act.: Klaus Wennemann, Barbara Rudnik, Nena, Benedict Freitag, Camilla Horn.
90 min.

## 1985 *Va Banque*

Three young people want to escape their financial dire straits by robbing an armored vehicle. They succeed, but then are blackmailed by an eyewitness.

Dir.: Diethard Küster.
SP.: Diethard Küster.
Cam.: Wolfgang Pilgrim.
Mus.: Achim Reichel, Toni Nissl.
Prod.: Fuzzi/Roxy.
Act.: Winfried Glatzeder, Grazyna Dylong, Achim Reichel, Claus-Dieter Reents, Joschka Fischer.
97 min.

## 1988 *Vatanyolu - Die Heimreise (Vatanyolu - The Voyage Home)*

Comedy in which a Turkish family decides to leave Germany and live in Turkey again, but on the way their car breaks down at the edge of a forest, and they decide just to stay there.

Dir.: Enis Günay, Rasim Konyar.
SP.: Enis Hünay, Rasim Konyar.
Cam.: Egon Werdin.
Mus.: Timur Selcuk.
Prod.: Franfurter Filmwerkstatt/ Pro-ject/E/R/Film.
Act.: Yaman Okay, Füsun Sen, Yavuz Kalan, Baris Cetinkaya, Jale Arikan.
94 min.

## 1988 *Die Venusfalle (Venus Trap)*

A young doctor, fearing the ties that bind, begins a search for the realization of all his dreams. When he finds the "perfect woman" of his secret fantasies, it results in some substantial changes.

Dir.: Robert Van Ackeren.
SP.: Robert Van Ackeren, Catharina Zwerenz.
Cam.: Jürgen Jürges.
Mus.: Peer Raben.
Prod.: Robert Van Ackeren Filmprod./M + P Film/Project/ZDF.
Act.: Horst-Günther Marx, Myriem Roussel, Sonja Kirchberger, Hanns Zischler, Rolf Zacher.
103 min.

1985 *Verbotene Träume (Forbidden Dreams)*

A patchwork of pornographic silent films from the twenties in Germany.

Edit.: Gerd Klein.
Mus.: Helge Schneider, Grieg, Handel, Mendelssohn-Bartholdy, Georges Bizet.
Prod.: Atlas.
95 min.

1989 *Verfolgte Wege (Paths Pursued)*

In the year 1946, a disturbed man returns from the war and finds a job in a small-town train station. He falls in love with a field-worker, and takes part in the theft of food packages, which leads to complications for him.

Dir.: Uwe Janson.
SP.: Uwe Janson.
Cam.: Egon Werdin.
Mus.: Michaela Dietl.
Prod.: Vulcano M.
Act.: Peter Cieslinski, Barbara Auer, Michael Dick, Tilo Prückner, Adolf Laimböck.
106 min.

1985 *Verführung: Die grausame Frau (Seduction: The Cruel Woman)*

An investigation in dramatic form of the tyranny of love and eroticism.

Dir/SP: Monika Treut, Elfi Mikesch.
Cam.: Elfi Mikesch.
Mus.: Marran Gosov.
Prod.: Hyäne I/II Filmprod. GbR, Berlin/Hamburg.
Act.: Mechthild Grossmann, Udo Kier, Sheila McLaughlin, Carola Regnier, Georgette Dee, Judith Flex, Barbara Ossenkopp.
85 min.

1988 *Vergessen Sie's (Forget It)*

A Hamburg taxi driver thinks he's found a body in a trash container. When no one seems to be interested in it, he begins his own investigation.

Dir.: C. Cay Wesnigk.
SP.: C. Cay Wesnigk.
Cam.: Bernd Meiners.
Mus.: Thomas Bauer.
Prod.: C. Cay Wesnigk Film/ZDF.
Act.: Edgar Marcus, Bernd Blasen, Necati Sahin, Sabine Hennemann, Werner Berndt.
80 min.

1987 (German-Yugoslavian) *Die Verliebten (Days to Remember)*

The love relationship between a female TV journalist and a composer, who is searching in Yugoslavia for clues to his father's Nazi past, ends in a deadly accident.

Dir.: Jeanine Meerapfel.
SP.: Jeanine Meerapfel.
Cam.: Pedrag Popovic.
Mus.: Jürgen Knieper.

Prod.:   Von Vietinghoff/Art Film 80/Zeta Film.
Act.:    Barbara Sukowa, Horst-Günther Marx, Beta
         Zivojinovic, Rade Serbedzija, Ljijala Kontic.
95 min.

### 1985-86  *Vermischte Nachrichten  (Mixed News)*

Collage film by Alexander Kluge, based on various stories from the
last page of a daily newspaper.

Dir.:    Alexander Kluge.
SP.:     Alexander Kluge.
Cam.:    Werner Lüring, Thomas Mauch.
Prod.:   Kairos-Film/ZDF.
Act.:    Marita Breuer, Rosel Zech, Sabine Wegner, Andre
         Jung, Sabine Trooger.
101 min.

### 1987  *Versteckte Liebe  (Hidden Love)*

A German dropout living on the island of Crete is brought out of his
exile by two children. He realizes that he is erotically attracted to the
eleven-year-old girl.

Dir.:    Gottfried Junker.
SP.:     Gottfried Junker.
Cam.:    Egon Werdin.
Mus.:    Chris Heyne.
Prod.:   Gottfried Junker/Pro-jekt/BR.
Act.:    Peter Cieslinski, Dimitra Spanou, Jorgos Balasis,
         Nikos Pektidou, Nektaria Nikolakakis.
79 min.

### 1985  *Der Videopirat  (Video Pirate)*

The struggle of an individual against an international dope-smuggling
and video-pirating organization.

Dir.:    Harald Alexander.

SP.:      Harald Alexander, Michael A. Berger.
Cam.:     Dietmar Garsoffky.
Mus.:     Detlef Wiese.
Prod.:    Cosmos.
Act.:     Nicolas Shopp, Maja Maranow, Werner
          Krumbiegel, Frank Trunz, Thomas Ullissner.
95 min.

1985  *40 qm Deutschland*  (*Forty Square Meters of Germany*)

A Turkish guest worker in Germany keeps his wife isolated in their gloomy apartment in order to keep a little piece of his culture alive in a foreign land.

Dir.:     Tevfik Baser.
SP.:      Tevfik Baser.
Cam.:     Izzet Akay.
Mus.:     Claus Bantzer.
Prod.:    Tevfik Baser/Studio Hamburg.
Act.:     Özay Fecht, Yaman Okay, Demir Gökgöl.
80 min.

1985-86  *Ein Virus kennt keine Moral*  (*A Virus has no Morals*)

Rosa von Praunheim shows the medical and political dangers of AIDS.

Dir.:     Rosa von Praunheim.
SP.:      Rosa von Praunheim.
Cam.:     Elfi Mikesch.
Mus.:     Maran Gosov.
Prod.:    Rosa von Praunheim Filmprod.
Act.:     Dieter Dicken, Maria Hasenäcker, Christian Kesten,
          Eva Kurz, Rosa von Praunheim.
82 min.

1985  *Voll auf der Rolle*  (*On a Roll*)

Berlin pupils rehearse the play "Stern ohne Himmel" ("Stars without a Sky"), in which some youths discover a Jewish boy hiding in a basement just before the end of World War II and are faced with the decision of what to do with him. The pupils bring their modern-day problems into play as they discuss who will play which roles.

Dir.:    Claudia Schröder, Detlef Gumm, Hans-Georg Ullrich.
SP.:     Leonie Ossowski.
Prod.:   Grips-Theater/Kinder- und Jugendfilmzentrum.
Act.:    Guntbert Warens, Ilona Schultz, Talcin Güzelce.
90 min.  (16 mm)

1986 (German-French) *Wahnfried - Richard & Cosima (Richard & Cosima)*

Scenes from the lives of Richard and Cosima Wagner, which show them celebrating, arguing and provoking one another.

Dir.: Peter Patzak.
SP.: Reinhard Baumgart.
Cam.: Toni Peschke.
Mus.: Carl Maria von Weber, Richard Wagner, Franz Liszt.
Prod.: Pro-jekt/SWF/Star.
Act.: Otto Sander, Tatja Seibt, Fabienne Babe, Peter Matic, Anton Diffring.
112 min.

1985 *Walkman Blues*

The everyday life of a young man living in Berlin, who is a musician and has a day job working for a wholesale butcher.

Dir.: Alfred Behrens.
SP.: Alfred Behrens.
Cam.: Claus Deubel.
Mus.: "Kraftwerk","Ludus","Blurt",Peter Radzuhn/Marius del Mestre, Heikko Deutschmann.
Prod.: Basis/ZDF/Channel Four.
Act.: Heikko Deutschmann, Jennifer Capraru, Madeleine Daevers, Jörg Körning, Sema Engin.
90 min.

1988 *Wallers letzter Gang (Waller's Last Trip)*

167

The railroad linesman, Waller, is about to make his last inspection; the train line is to be shut down. As he walks along the tracks, he also journeys through the memories of his life, all somehow connected to this track in this valley.

Dir.:　　Christian Wagner.
SP.:　　Christian Wagner, from a novel by Gerhard Köpf.
Cam.:　Thomas Mauch.
Mus.:　Florian E. Müller.
Prod.:　Christian Wagner Filmprod./BR.
Act.:　 Rolf Illig, Herbert Knaup, Sibylle Canonica, Crescentia Dünßer, Franz Boehm.
100 min.

1987 *Wann, wenn nicht jetzt? (When, if Not Now?)*

An elderly professor and his wife return to the Federal Republic of Germany after having lived for forty years in the U.S. No sooner are they back than the old rivalry between the professor and his wife's previous beau flares up again, this time over a young nurse.

Dir.:　　Michael Juncker.
SP.:　　Michael Juncker, Doris Dörrie.
Cam.:　Helge Weindler.
Mus.:　Claus Bantzer.
Prod.:　Olga-Film/ZDF.
Act.:　 Hans Peter Hallwachs, Friedrich von Thun, Hannelore Schroth, Gudrun Gabriel, Elma Karlowa.
99 min.

1986 *War Zone - Todeszone (War Zone - Death Zone)*

An American TV journalist lands an interview with the alleged leaders of the PLO in Beirut, and winds up getting involved in the intrigues between the Palestinians and the Falangists.

Dir.:　　Nathaniel Gutman.
SP.:　　Hanan Peled, Nathaniel Gutman.
Cam.:　Amnon Salomon, Thomas Mauch.

Mus.:    Jacques Zwart, Hans Jansen.
Prod.:   Creative Film/Caro Film/NDR.
Act.:    Christopher Walken, Marita Marschall, Hywel
         Bennett, Arnon Zadok, Amos Lavie.
99 min.

1987 *Warten auf Marie* (*Waiting for Marie*)

Several people waiting for a baby to be born are confronted with
their own spiritual and philosophical positions.

Dir.:    Gisela Stelly.
SP.:     Gisela Stelly, Harald Vogl.
Cam.:    Bernd Fiedler.
Mus.:    Janina Milota, Patrick Korn.
Prod.:   Stelly-Filmprod./Hamburger Wirtschaftsförderung.
Act.:    Eva Marie Hagen, Hermann Lause, Nele
         Fleischmann, Felix Reidenbach, Hildegard Schmahl.
82 min.

1989 *Wedding* (*Wedding*)

Three friends from the working-class district of Wedding in North
Berlin meet up again after not having seen one another for several
years. In spending a day and a night with one another, they catch up
on all they have done and not done during that time.

Dir.:    Heiko Schier.
SP.:     Heiko Schier.
Cam.:    Jörg Jeshel.
Mus.:    Piet Klocke.
Prod.:   Metropolis.
Act.:    Angela Schmid-Burgk, Roger Hübner, Harald
         Kempe, Heino Ferch, Wolfgang Bathke.
87 min.

1988 *Die weißen Zwerge* (*The White Dwarfs*)

A young couple in Berlin live their daily routines.  For her, a supermarket checker, everything is fine; for him, a cook, boredom is setting in. When he suddenly falls ill and dies, she has no trouble at all finding another man to fit into her routine.

Dir.: Dirk Schäfer.
SP.: Dirk Schäfer, Patricia Kalmar.
Cam.: Ernst Kubitza.
Mus.: J.S. Bach.
Prod.: Tara-Film Scheuver-Gartell, Berlin/ZDF.
Act.: Nirit Sommerfeld, Michael Schech, Julia Lindig, Hussi Kutlucan, Thomas Schlechter.
75 min.

1986 (German-Austrian) *Das weite Land* *(The Vast Land)*

In Vienna at the turn of the century, an egotistical gigolo and a man unhappy in love manage to convince a married woman to avoid the temptations of upper-class fashionability.

Dir.: Luc Bondy.
SP.: Lubor Meir Donhal, Luc Bondy, from a play by Arthur Schnitzler.
Cam.: Thomas Mauch.
Mus.: Heinz Leonhardsberger.
Prod.: Almaro/Arabella/WDR/Antenne 2/RAI II.
Act.: Michel Piccoli, Bulle Ogier, Dominique Blanc, Alain Cuny, Jutta Lampe.
103 min.

1985 (Austrian-German-Swiss) *Welcome in Vienna*

An Austrian emigrant returns to Vienna in 1945 along with a unit of the U.S. Army responsible for psychological warfare. The former emigrant attempts to find a new niche for himself in the new situation in Austria.

Dir.: Axel Corti.
SP.: Georg Stefan Troller, Axel Corti.
Cam.: Gernot Roll.

Mus.:   Hans Georg Koch, Alban-Berg-Quartett.
Prod.:  Thalia Film/ORF/ZDF/SRG.
Act.:   Gabriel Barylli, Nicolas Brieger, Claudia Messner,
        Joachim Kemmer, Karl-Heinz Hackl.
127 min.

### 1989-90  *Werner - Beinhart!*  *(Werner)*

The unsuccessful cartoonist Brösel has a chance to make it big when
his comic strip, Werner, is going to be made into a movie.

Dir.:   Niki List (real), Michael Schaack, Gerd Hahn
        (animation segments).
SP.:    Ernst Kahl, Werner "Brösel" Feldmann, from a
        comic strip by "Brösel."
Cam.:   Egon Werdin.
Mus.:   Jörg Evers, "Torfrock."
Prod.:  Neue Constantin.
Act.:   Rötger "Brösel" Feldmann, Meret Becker, I. Stangl,
        Ludger Pistor, Johannes Silberschneider.
93 min.

### 1985  *Westler  (Westerners)*

Felix returns to West Berlin from Los Angeles, then visits East
Berlin, where he meets the homosexual Thomas, and the two plan a
trip together to Prague, where Thomas plans to attempt an escape to
the West.

Dir.:   Wieland Speck.
SP.:    Wieland Speck, Egbert Hörmann.
Cam.:   Klemens Becker, Klaus Krieger.
Mus.:   Engelbert Rehm.
Prod.:  Searcher Filmproduction Sunger & Grüttgen/ZDF.
Act.:   Sigurd Rachmann, Rainer Strecker, Andy Lucas,
        Andreas Bernhardt, Sascha Hammer.
94 min.

### 1986  *Whopper-Punch 777*

Comedy in which Otto Paletti, Jr. attempts to fill in for his father, a famed sports reporter, and interview the great boxer Billy "Whopper" Punch.

| | |
|---|---|
| Dir.: | Jürgen Tröster. |
| SP.: | Maria Axt, from a children's book by Maria Axt. |
| Cam.: | Michael Teutsch. |
| Mus.: | Matthias Brendel. |
| Prod.: | Tröster Film/Roxy. |
| Act.: | Burkhard Rönnefarth, Manfred Krug, Günter Kaufmann, Hans-Halmut Dickow, Barbara Czerwinski. |
| 68 min. | |

1986  *Wie treu ist Nik?  (How Loyal is Nik?)*

A star causes his record company a lot of trouble when he announces to the world that he no longer loves everyone, but just loves one woman.

| | |
|---|---|
| Dir.: | Eckhart Schmidt. |
| SP.: | Eckhart Schmidt. |
| Cam.: | Bernd Neubauer. |
| Mus.: | Sal Paradise. |
| Prod.: | Wolfgang Odenthal Film/Raphaela Film. |
| Act.: | Sal Paradise, Stefanie Petsch, Sibylle Rauch, Antje Hirsch, Ursula Karven. |
| 83 min. | |

1989  (French-German-English)  *Der wiedergefundene Freund  (The Re-Found Friend)*

In 1932, a Jewish boy had begun a friendship with the son of an aristocratic family. Sixty years later, the man searches for the friend of his youth, their friendship having been destroyed by the circumstances of the Nazi era.

| | |
|---|---|
| Dir.: | Jerry Schatzberg. |
| SP.: | Harold Pinter, from a novel by Fred Uhlman. |

Cam.: Bruno de Keyzer.
Mus.: Philippe Sarde.
Prod.: Les Film Ariane/FR e/NEF/Maran/Arbo/C.L.G.
Act.: Jason Robards, Christian Anholt, Samuel West, Francoise Fabian, Barbara Jefford.
110 min.

## 1985 *Der wilde Clown (The Wild Clown)*

In his search for his lost homeland, a worker from the upper Palatinate flees with a few close friends to a shot-up building at the military practice field. Here, they attempt to fulfill their dreams of living a free life.

Dir.: Josef Rödl.
SP.: Josef Rödl.
Cam.: Charly Gschwind.
Mus.: Eberhard Schoener.
Prod.: Bavaria/Josef Rödl-Filmprod./ZDF.
Act.: Sigi Zimmerschied, Sunnyi Melles, Peter Kern, Ivo Vrzal-Wiegand, Ursula Strätz.
103 min.

## 1990 *Winckelmanns Reisen (Oh Rosa!)*

Ernst Winckelmann, a shampoo salesman in Schleswig-Holstein, lives in the past, which makes his contemporary relationships suffer. One day, his ex-wife appears on the scene with their five-year-old daughter, whom he did not know existed, and he is to care for her for the day.

Dir.: Jan Schütte.
SP.: Jan Schütte, Thomas Strittmatter.
Cam.: Sophie Maintigneux.
Mus.: Claus Bantzer.
Prod.: Novoskop/Pandora/WDR.
Act.: Wolf-Dietrich Sprenger, Susanne Lother, Traugott Buhre, Mathias Gnädinger, Mine-Marei Wiegandt.
80 min.

1988 (Polish-German-Italian-French) *Wo immer du bist (Wherever You Are)*

In 1938, a young German diplomat and businessman returns from Uruguay to take over a factory in Poland. While his wife suffers from the signs of impending war, he refuses to see the symptoms until it is too late.

> Dir.: Krzysztof Zanussi.
> SP.: Krzysztof Zanussi.
> Cam.: Slawomir Idziak.
> Mus.: Wojciech Kilar.
> Prod.: Zespoly Filmowe/Gerhard Schmidt Filmprod./Challenge Film Enzo Petri/Marie-Francoise Mascaro/La Sept.
> Act.: Julian Sands, Renee Soutendijk, Joachim Krol, Milva, Maciej Robakiewicz.
> 112 min.

## 1987 *Wohin? (Where To?)*

A movie by Herbert Achternbusch that appeals for humanity and dignity for those who have contracted AIDS.

> Dir.: Herbert Achternbusch.
> SP.: Herbert Achternbusch.
> Cam.: Adam Olech.
> Mus.: Tom Waits.
> Prod.: Herbert Achternbusch.
> Act.: Herbert Achternbusch, Gabi Geist, Annamirl Bierbichler, Franz Baumgartner, Kurt Raab.
> 96 min.

## 1984-85 *Die Wolfsbraut (The Wolf's Bride)*

The brief friendship between a female film director, who is experiencing for the first time the humiliation of being unemployed, and a young foreign woman who works in a movie theater as the cleaning lady.

Dir.:   Dagmar Beiersdorf.
SP.:    Dagmar Beiersdorf.
Cam.:   Christoph Gies.
Mus.:   Pete Wyoming-Bender, Albert Kittler, A.M.
        Hildegrandt.
Prod.:  Dagmar Beiersdorf/NDF.
Act.:   Imke Barnstedt, Martine Felton, Lothar Lambert,
        Albert Heins, Mustafa Iskandarani.
85 min.

1990  *Wonderbeat*

A low-budget production highlighting the popular German rock band
of the 1960s, the "Rattles."

Dir.:   Claude-Oliver Rudolph.
SP.:    Claude-Oliver Rudolph.
Cam.:   Otto Kirchhoff.
Mus.:   Miro Nemec, Claude-Oliver Rudolph, Uwe
        Fellensiek, The Wonderbeats.
Prod.:  Wild Movie/Claude-Oliver Rudolph.
Act.:   Richy Müller, Jürgen Vogel, Uwe Fellensiek, Ralph
        Richter, Sabine von Maydell.
91 min.

1981  (German-Hungarian)  *Wuk, der Fuchs  (Wuk the Fox)*

Cartoon film of the adventures of a little fox.

Dir.:   Attila Dargay.
SP.:    Attila Dargay, Istvan Imre, Ede Tarbay, from a
        novel by Istvan Fekete.
Cam.:   Iren Henrik.
Mus.:   Peter Wolf.
Prod.:  Infafilm/Hungarofilm (Pannonia Filmstudio).
85 min.

## 1985 *Xaver*

A naive village youth finds a friend in a gnome-like extra-terrestrial being, who helps him fight off a biker gang and the villagers who taunt him.

Dir.: Werner Possardt.
SP.: Werner Possardt.
Cam.: Jakob Eger.
Mus.: Hans Jürgen Buchner, Haindling.
Prod.: Calypso.
Act.: Rupert Seidl, Carlos Pavlidis, Gabi Fischer, Marinus Brand, Heinz Josef Braun.
90 min.

1987-88  *Yasemin*

A seventeen-year-old Turkish girl falls in love with a German boy and comes into conflict with her father and all the traditions he still believes in.

Dir.:   Hark Bohm.
SP.:    Hark Bohm.
Cam.:   Slawomir Idziak.
Mus.:   Hans Peter Ostendorf.
Prod.:  Hamburger Kino Kompanie/ZDF.
Act.:   Ayse Romey, Uwe Bohm, Senner Sen, Ilhan Emirli,
        Katharina Lehmann.
86 min.

## 1987 z.B. ... *Otto Spalt* (e.g. ... *Otto Spalt*)

Satire in which a committee of the Film Promotion Board *(Filmförderungsanstalt)* is assigned the task of evaluating whether a director's film should be financially supported. The committee attempts to do this only by viewing several of his short films.

Dir.: Rene Perraudin.
SP.: Rene Perraudin.
Cam.: Werner Nitschke.
Mus.: Klaus Doldinger.
Prod.: Filmprod. Rene Perraudin.
Act.: Otto Sander, Alfred Edel, Rold Zacher, Katharina Thalbach, Heinz Meier.
100 min.

## 1986 *Zabou*

Detective Schimanski investigates a drug ring, and while doing so meets up with his foster daughter whom he has not seen in years. It soon appears that she is connected with the crack ring.

Dir.: Hajo Gies.
SP.: Martin Gies, Axel Götz.
Cam.: Axel Block.
Mus.: Klaus Lage.
Prod.: Bavaria/Neue Constantin/WDR.
Act.: Götz George, Claudia Messmer, Wolfram Berger, Hannes Jaenicke, Eberhard Feik.
102 min.

## 1985 *Zahn um Zahn (A Tooth for a Tooth)*

After being suspended from duty, Inspector Schimanski solves a complicated murder case single-handedly.

Dir.: Hajo Gies.
SP.: Horst Vocks, Thomas Wittenberg.
Cam.: Jürgen Jürges.
Mus.: Klaus Lage Band.
Prod.: Bavaria/Neue Constantin/WDR.
Act.: Götz George, Renan Demirkan, Rufus, Eberhard Feik, Charles Brauer.
95 min.

1987 *Zärtliche Chaoten (Lovable Zanies)*

Three men fall in love with the same woman, and things get interesting when she announces she's pregnant.

Dir.: Franz Josef Gottlieb.
SP.: Thomas Gottschalk.
Cam.: Klaus Werner.
Prod.: Lisa/K.S.
Act.: Thomas Gottschalk, Helmut Fischer, Michael Winslow, Dey Young, Pierre Brice.
93 min.

1988 *Zärtliche Chaoten II (Three Crazy Jerks 2)*

With the aid of a time machine, two men attempt to prevent the birth of their boss.

Dir.: Thomas Gottschalk, Holm Dressler.
SP.: Thomas Gottschalk.
Cam.: Atze Glanert.
Prod.: K.S. Film/Roxy-Film.
Act.: Thomas Gottschalk, Helmut Fischer, Michael Winslow, Deborah Shelton, Harald Leipnitz.
96 min.

## 1987 *Die Zeit des Birkenjungen (The Days of the Birchboy)*

A young boy, abandoned by his mother, has the image of a lone birch tree ingrained in his memory. He grows up in an orphanage, and later becomes a famous automobile designer. When he decides to search for his mother, he finds her working in a bordello, and both regret the lives they have lived without each other's love.

> Dir.: Elld Antonio Schott.
> SP.: Elld Antonio Schott.
> Cam.: Elld Antonio Schott.
> Mus.: Gert Wilden, Franz Titscher.
> Prod.: Bernd International Movie.
> Act.: Marlies Schoenau, Dominik Hamerstein, Hans Peter Duerr, Jan Krueger, Michael Grube.
> 96 min.

## 1985 *Ein Zirkus voller Abenteuer (A Circus Full of Adventure)*

The Ministry for Youth from the city of Unna organized a three-week circus tour for children from foster families and orphanages. The children were taught how to perform some of their own circus acts.

> Dir.: Detlef Gumm, Hans-Georg Ullrich.
> SP.: · Detlef Gumm, Hans-Georg Ullrich.
> 80 min. (16 mm)

## 1986 *Zischke*

When a young Berlin boy's mother leaves him alone for a few days, he attempts to leave Berlin to search for his father in Italy.

> Dir.: Martin Theo Krieger.
> SP.: Martin Theo Krieger.
> Cam.: Claus Deubel.
> Mus.: Barbara Thompson.
> Prod.: Backhaus + Krieger Filmprod.
> Act.: David Strempel, Amira Ghazala, Darja Lingenberg,

Knut Rauter, Ilona Lewanowski.
93 min.

## 1985-6 *Zoning*

In a gigantic skyscraper with a high-tech security system, two disillusioned burglars break in and rob the inhabitants.

Dir.:   Ulrich Krenkler.
SP.:    Angelika Hacker, Ulrich Krenkler.
Cam.:   Nikolaus Starkmeth.
Mus.:   Tangerine Dream.
Prod.:  Scala.
Act.:   Hubertus Gertzen, Norbert Lamla, Veronika Wolff, Dieter Meier, Eleonore Weisberger.
91 min.

## 1988 *Zugzwang (Fool's Mate)*

A once-famous pianist has fallen on hard times and becomes more and more addicted to gambling, destroying his family fortune as well as his career.

Dir.:   Mathieu Carriere.
SP.:    Mathieu Carriere.
Cam.:   Rolf Liccini.
Mus.:   Klaus Buhlert.
Prod.:  von Vietinghoff/ZDF.
Act.:   Michael Marwitz, Victoria Tennant, Maria Barranco, Stuart Wilson, Clayton George.
95 min.

## 1989 *Zwei Frauen (Silence like Glass)*

An attractive young ballerina learns that she has cancer; when she meets another young woman who also has cancer but a totally different personality from her own, she derives a great deal of strength from her new friendship.

Dir.:    Carl Schenkel.
SP.:     Bea Hellmann, Carl Schenkel.
Cam.:    Dietrich Lohmann.
Mus.:    Anne Dudley.
Prod.:   Bavaria/Roxy/Lisa.
Act.:    Jami Gertz, Martha Plimpton, George Peppard, Bruce Payre, Rip Torn.
103 min.

1985  *Die zwei Gesichter des Januar  (The Two Faces of January)*

A young American witnesses a crime but gets hopelessly involved with the criminal in a deadly fight for the love of the criminal's wife.

Dir.:    Wolfgang Storch.
SP.:     Karl-Heinz Willschrei, Wolfgang Storch, from a novel by Patricia Highsmith.
Cam.:    Wolfgang Treu.
Mus.:    Eberhard Schoener.
Prod.:   Monaco/Süddeutscher Rundfunk.
Act.:    Yolande Gilot, Charles Brauer, Thomas Schücke.
113 min.

1987  (French-German)  *Zwei halbe Helden  (Fucking Fernand)*

Black comedy in which a blind male virgin and a smalltime hood are thrown together in occupied France, where they jolt from adventure to adventure.

Dir.:    Gerard Mordillat.
SP.:     Vera Belmont, Jean Aurenche.
Cam.:    Jean Monsigny.
Mus.:    Jean-Claude Petit.
Prod.:   Stephan Film/I.C.E./Delta.
Act.:    Thierry Lhermitte, Jean Yanne, Marie Laforet, Charlotte Valandrey, Hark Bohm.
81 min.

1986  *Zweikampf (Duel)*

The plot centers on a duel between a retired man who murders to be
left alone and a retired detective who tries to catch him.

> Dir.:    Gert Steinheimer.
> SP.:     Gert Steinheimer.
> Cam.:    Immo Rentz.
> Mus.:    Klaus Nagel.
> Prod.:   SWF/NDR.
> Act.:    Joachim  Wichmann,  Adolf  Laimböck,  Heiner
>          Kollhoff, Ernst Konarek, Roland Kenda.
> 83 min.

# BIOGRAPHIES - DIRECTORS

The following section contains basic biographical information on major West German directors who made feature films between 1985 and 1991, unless they have already been included in our original volume, *West German Cinema since 1945: A Reference Handbook* (Scarecrow Press, 1987). For individual films of these directors, all of which are listed in the filmography, see the alphabetical index of names at the end of the book.

ADLON, Percy. Born in 1935, grew up in Ammerland and the Starnberg Lake district south of Munich. Studied German literature, drama, and art history. Began acting career in the university drama group. Has had an extensive career as theater actor, has written radio plays, and made documentary films. Since the early 1980s, he has been primarily involved in feature film directing.

AGTHE, Arend. Born in 1949 in Rastede (near Oldenburg). Studied German literature, art history, and philosophy at the University of Marburg. Made short films and worked for the magazine *Pardon* from 1972-74. Completed his university degree (*Staatsexamen*) in 1975.

BALLMANN, Herbert. Born in 1924 in Dortmund. Was assistant director for DEFA (East Germany) in the early 1950s, then director in his own right there until moving to West Germany in 1959. Since then, he has been involved in theater, television, and film directing.

BANNERT, Walter. Born in 1942 in Vienna, the son of a working-class family. After completing an electrician's apprenticeship, he began a career as a photographer and cameraman. As a short filmmaker, he was a leader of the young Austrian film movement of the 70s. Since the late 70s, he has primarily made feature films.

**BASER, Tevfik.** Born in 1951 in Turkey, completed school there in 1970, then spent five years in London. Trained in Turkey as a graphic artist, stage designer, photographer, and cameraman. In Hamburg since 1980, he studied at the Art Institute there. He made documentary films before directing his first feature film in 1988.

**BEIERSDORF, Dagmar.** Born in 1946, studied drama and journalism, and began as an assistant director and actress in television and movies. Since 1977 she has been directing in her own right.

**BLUMENBERG, Hans-Christoph.** Born in 1947, grew up in Bremen, studied history and German literature in Cologne. From 1966 to 1983 he was film critic in Cologne for the *Stadt-Anzeiger* and in Hamburg for *Die Zeit.* After making documentary films for television, he began his career as feature filmmaker in 1984.

**BOHM, Hark.** Born in 1939, completed law studies in 1966. Co-founder of the *Filmverlag der Autoren* in 1970, with Wim Wenders, Rainer Werner Fassbinder, Peter Lilienthal, Thomas Schamoni, and others. Occasional film roles in Fassbinder's films, then director/actor in his own feature films from 1971 on.

**BÖLL, Christoph.** Born in 1949 in Cologne, studied at the University of Bochum. Made two dozen "self-produced" films before beginning as television and movie director in the early 1980s.

**BRASCH, Thomas.** Born in 1945 in Yorkshire, England, the son of Jewish emigrants from Germany. In 1947, the family returned to East Germany. After high school, he worked as a typesetter and mechanic before beginning journalism study in Leipzig. Expelled from the university for criticizing political leaders in the GDR, he began filmmaking studies at the DEFA film school in Potsdam in 1966. In 1968, he was accused of seditious activities and sentenced to 27 months in jail. After serving his sentence, he worked as a free-lance writer before being asked to leave the GDR in 1956. He lives in Berlin, where he began his career as a film director in 1977.

BRINGMANN, Peter. Born in Hannover in 1946, studied at the College of Television and Cinema in Munich from 1968-71. Worked as director and production supervisor, gained experience also as scriptwriter. He has been making feature films since the early 1980s.

BRÜCKNER, Jutta. Born in Düsseldorf in 1941, studied philosophy, political science, and history in Berlin, Paris, and Munich. Completed her doctorate in political science in 1973 at the University of Munich. Experience in script and radio play writing, all aspects of filmmaking, also film journalism. She teaches film at the German Film and Television Academy in Berlin.

BÜLD, Wolfgang. Born in 1952 in Lüdenscheid, studied at the College of Television and Cinema in Munich from 1974-77. He has worked as writer, documentary filmmaker, and he has produced music videos.

BUSCHMANN, Christel. Studied German literature, romance languages, and philosophy in Hamburg, Montreal, and Munich. She is a literary critic and has taught at the German Film and Television Academy in Berlin, at the Comprehensive College in Kassel, and at the College of Television and Cinema in Munich. First worked in film as a script author, then as director.

CARRIERE, Mathieu. Born in Hannover in 1950, engaged in international cinema and television productions since his school days. Established as a theater and film actor, author, producer, and director, as well as roles in operas and variety shows.

CLAUS, Richard. Born in 1950 in Kassel, graduated from the German Film and Television Academy in Berlin, where he still lives. Work in animation, documentary film, and feature film as writer and director.

DÖRRIE, Doris. Born in Hannover in 1955, studied theater and film in California and New York from 1973-75, then at the College of Television and Cinema in Munich from 1975-78. Early work as scriptwriter and in documentary filmmaking before turning to feature films in the 1980s.

EDEL, Uli. Born in Neuenburg (Rhine) in 1947, he studied theater and German literature before completing film training at the College of Television and Cinema in Munich from 1970-73. Works in television and feature filmmaking.

EMMERICH, Roland. Born in Stuttgart in 1955, attended the Stuttgart Academy of Art and worked on animated films as well as in advertising. Studied film at the College of Television and Cinema in Munich from 1977 on, has occasionally worked as an actor. Since the early 1980s involved primarily in feature film directing.

ENGSTRÖM, Ingemo. Born in Finnland of Swedish-Finnish parents, studied psychology, medicine, and literature in Helsinki, then Hamburg and Munich. Completed studies at the College of Television and Cinema in Munich in 1970 and has made feature films since the early 1970s.

ERLER, Rainer. Born in Munich in 1933, early work as assistant director with Braun, Hoffmann, Verhoeven, Liebeneiner, worked as writer, director, and producer for Bavaria Studios in Munich.

FISCHER, Markus. Born in Zurich in 1953, made short films in the 1970s before beginning a career as producer, scriptwriter, director, and film score composer. He has produced music videos as well as feature films since the early 1980s.

**FRANK, Hubert.** Born in southern Moravia in 1925, worked as writer, journalist, editor, and director. More than thirty feature films, some of which have achieved popularity in other European countries.

**FRANKENBERG, Pia.** Born in Cologne in 1957, attended acting school. She began her film career in the late 1970s and was a writer, assistant director, producer. Since the mid-1980s, she has been making her own feature films.

**FRATSCHER, Peter.** Born in Kassel in 1950, studied German literature, philosophy, and sociology in Frankfurt before completing film training at the College of Television and Cinema in Munich from 1971-74.

**FRIEßNER, Uwe.** Born in 1942, studied German literature and philosophy in Berlin. Worked occasionally on deep-sea fishing crew, also as a roofer before completing film studies at the German Film and Television Academy in Berlin fom 1975-78.

**GIES, Hajo.** Born in 1945 in Lüdenscheid, studied in Frankfurt before going to the College of Television and Cinema in Munich. Extensive work in television as director (*"Tatort"*).

**GRAF, Dominik.** Born in 1952 in Munich. He studied German literature and musicology, then began his film training at the College of Television and Cinema in Munich in 1974. Worked as actor and writer at Bavaria Studios in Munich, then in television before beginning his career as a feature film director in the early 1980s.

**HAFFTER, Petra.** Studied journalism, theater, and political science in Berlin. Worked as a writer for radio, made documentary and television films. Since the early 1980s active as producer and director of feature films.

**HAMOS, Gusztav.** Born in Budapest in 1955, completed film training at the German Film and Television Academy in Berlin. Several video feature films before turning to film in the mid-1980s.

**HERBRICH, Oliver.** Born in Munich in 1961, received a script stipend at the age of eighteen and completed his first feature film in 1980 before graduating from the *Gymnasium*. Studied at the College of Television and Cinema in Munich.

**HOFMANN, Nico.** Born in Heidelberg in 1959, studied from 1980 to 1985 at the College of Television and Cinema in Munich. He has made feature films since the mid-1980s.

**HUETTNER, Ralf.** Born in Munich in 1954, began studying to become a sculptor, then went to the College of Television and Cinema in Munich in the early 1980s. Since 1985 he has made feature films.

**KEGLEVIC, Peter.** Born in Salzburg in 1950, trained as a bookseller before studying at the *Mozarteum* from 1970-74. After work in theater and television, he directed his first feature film in 1982.

**KERN, Peter.** Born in Vienna in 1949, sang in the Vienna Boy's Choir. Extensive experience as actor in feature and television films, including winning several acting prizes, and also as a producer. His debut as a director came in the mid-1980s.

**KLÖCKNER, Beate.** Born in Koblenz in 1950, trained as a bookseller, then completed university studies. After working as a writer and free-lance journalist, she amassed experience as an assistant director in the theater, and she has also taught at the University of Frankfurt. She began her feature film career in the early 1980s.

**KNILLI, Maria.** Born in Graz (Austria) in 1959, spent part of her youth in Berlin. Worked as a reporter in Austria before going to the College of Television and Cinema in Munich from 1979-83. Experience as a film editor and writer, filmmaker since the early 1980s.

**KONERMANN, Lutz.** Born in the Rhineland in 1958, completed school in Milan, then studied at the College of Television and Cinema in Munich from 1977-82. Has worked as a cameraman, as a director of feature films since 1983.

**KRIEGER, Martin Theo.** Born in Lingen (Ems) in 1953, studied music pedagogy and theater in Hildesheim and Berlin. After studies at the German Film and Television Academy in Berlin (1981-83), work as camera and sound man in television and film. His first feature film was made in 1986.

**LAMBERT, Lothar.** Born in Rudolstadt (Thuringia) in 1944, grew up in Berlin. After studying journalism and working as a journalist, he turned to writing film reviews. His own filmmaking career began in the early 1970s.

**LEVY, Dani.** Born in Basel in 1957, actor and author in the Basel Youth Theater from 1977-79, then a member of the *Rote Grütze* theater in Berlin. Television series acting, writing, some radio writing. Feature filmmaking since the mid-1980s.

**MEERAPFEL, Jeanine.** Daughter of German-Jewish emigrants, grew up in Argentina. She has lived in the Federal Republic since 1964 and studied filmmaking with Alexander Kluge from 1964-68 in Ulm. She worked as a film critic, also made short films and documentary films in the 1960s and 1970s, and began making feature films in the early 1980s.

**MIEHE, Ulf.** (See interview with him in our first volume, *West German Cinema since 1945 - A Reference Handbook*, pp. 12-15. Ulf Miehe died on July 13, 1989 in Munich.)

**MITTERMAYR, Berthold.** Born in Linz (Austria) in 1952, studied chemistry in Vienna before coming to the United States in 1972/73, where he worked as a dishwasher, cook, and bodyguard. Began study of film at the College of Television and Cinema in Munich in the late 1970s, worked as cameraman and writer. Has made his own feature films since the early 1980s.

MÜLLERSCHÖN, Niki. Born in Stuttgart in 1958, began acting during school years. Various film activities (camera, sound, assistant director) before making first feature films for German television. Several commercial feature films since the mid-1980s.

NÜCHTERN, Rüdiger. Born 1945, studied theater history and German literature before beginning film study at College of Television and Cinema in Munich in 1968. Founding member of the *Filmverlag der Autoren*, directed several television movies before starting feature film career in the early 1980s.

PATZAK, Peter. Born in 1945 in Vienna, came to the U. S. to work for a television station after briefly studying psychology and art history. Several years working in television in Austria, began his feature film career in the mid-1970s.

POHLAND, Hansjürgen. Born in Berlin in 1934, studied music, then began to learn the film trade at the *Mosaik film editing and copying center*. *He made twenty-one short films before beginning his feature film career as a producer in the early 1960s.*

PRÖTTL, Dr. Dieter. *Born in 1933 in Offenburg, completed business degree, then a doctorate in 1961. Worked in cabaret, television, film, then as a television editor and director in* Baden-Baden. He has concentrated on feature films, especially comedies, from the mid-1980s on.

RATEUKE, Christian. Born in 1943 in Berlin, training as assistant director at the *Forum* theater in Berlin, then co-director in Bremen. He began his film career in the late 1970s.

**RIPPLOH, Frank.** After beginning a career as a schoolteacher, he made a name for himself with a self-produced slide presentation devoted to the private lives of teachers. He made his first feature film in 1981 (*Taxi zum Klo*).

**RÖDL, Josef.** Born in 1949 in the Palatinate, he was first trained as an auto mechanic, then came to the College of Television and Cinema in Munich in the early 1970s. His first feature films were made in the late 1970s.

**ROSENBAUM, Marianne S. W.** Born in 1940 in Bohemia, she studied painting in Munich, later beginning a study of cinema in Prague and Munich. Co-director of successful television series, then documentary film work and feature films, beginning in the early 1980s.

**SALESS, Sohrab Shahid.** Born in 1944 in Teheran, he has lived in the Federal Republic since 1974. He studied theater direction in Vienna and Paris, worked for the Iranian Ministry of Culture and Art before beginning his feature film career in the early 1970s.

**SCHENKEL, Carl.** Born in Bern in 1948, he studied theater and journalism in Berlin. After stints as director's assistant with Staudte, Geissendörfer, and others, he made documentaries. His first feature films came in the early 1980s.

**SCHMIDT, Eckhart.** Born in 1939, he was a film critic for many years before beginning to make feature films in 1968. After a break of more then ten years from filmmaking, he returned in the early 1980s and made half a dozen films in the 1980s.

**SCHRADER, Uwe.** Born in 1954, he studied at the German Film and Television Academy in Berlin. After several successful short and documentary films, he began to make feature films in the early 1980s.

**SCHRÖDER, Claudia.** Born in 1953 in Lauenburg/Elbe, studied art education and sociology in the early 1970s. After working for two years as a free-lance television journalist in the late 1970s, she worked as assistant director and began her feature film directing career in 1982.

SCHÜTTE, Jan. Born in 1957 in Mannheim, studied literature and art history in Tübingen, Zurich, and Hamburg, then worked as a journalist on newspapers and in television. He began making documentaries in the early 1980s, then directed his first feature film in 1987 (*Drachenfutter*).

SCHWABENITZKY, Reinhard. Born in 1947 in Austria, studied film in Vienna for eight semesters, completing a diploma in camera and directing. After work as assistant director (Wicki, Corti, Glück), he began making feature films for television and movie theaters in the mid-1970s.

SCHWARZENBERGER, Xaver. Born in 1946 in Vienna, worked first as a cameraman on more than thirty documentaries for Austrian and Bavarian television. Moved to Munich in 1979, worked with R. W. Fassbinder on the latter's *Berlin Alexanderplatz*, among several other films, then began his own directing career in the mid-1980s.

STEINER, Rudolf. Born in Berlin in 1942, graduated from the DEFA (East German) film academy in Potsdam-Babelsberg. He worked as a cameraman for East German television until coming to the west in early 1971. Feature films beginning in 1973.

SYDOW, Rolf von. Born in 1924 in Wiesbaden, worked as radio play director for RIAS (*Radio im amerikanischen Sektor*) in Berlin before going into television directing. He did not make his first feature films until the early 1980s.

TIMM, Peter. Born in 1950 in Berlin, studied history and Russian at the Humboldt University, then theater at the Berlin School of Drama. After a jail sentence for dissident activities (1972-73), he was expelled from the GDR and settled in the west.

His feature film career began in the early 1980s.

**TREUT, Monika.** Born in 1954, studied literature and semiotics in Marburg, completing her doctorate in 1983. After work in video, she began to make documentaries and occasional feature films.

**VILSMAIER, Joseph.** Born in Munich in 1939, he was trained as a camerman and worked for the Bavaria studios for several years before making his first feature films in the 1980s.

**WEISS, Jiri.** Born in 1913 in Prague, studied law and worked as a journalist before making his first film in 1935. He emigrated to England in 1939 and worked there as a documentary filmmaker. In 1945 he returned to Czechoslovakia and became one of the leaders of their cinema. He came to the U. S. in 1968 and has lived here since, teaching at the University of California/Santa Barbara and New York University.

**WICKER, Wigbert.** Born in 1939 in Allendorf (Marburg), studied English and German in Marburg, Munich, and Ediburgh. He worked as assistant director (Vohrer, Wirth, Don Taylor), then began his own feature film directing career in the early 1970s.

**WINKELMANN, Adolf.** Born in 1946 in Hallenberg (Westphalia), studied art in Kassel before beginning his cinema career with 16 mm. films in the mid-1960s. After documentaries and television work, he began his own feature film career in the late 1970s.

**WOLFSPERGER, Douglas.** Born in 1958 in Zurich, grew up in Germany in Constance and Friedrichshafen. Training as television director in Baden-Baden, then he studied theater and musicology in Munich. His first feature film appeared in 1985.

# INDEX OF DIRECTORS

Names in parentheses indicate pseudonyms or real names, respectively. Spelling variations commonly used in German:

ä = ae;  ö = oe;  ü = ue;  ß = ss.

Abbrescia-Rath, Silvana 103
Achternbusch, Herbert  48, 64, 66, 103, 118, 174
Adlon, Percy  114, 125
Agthe, Arend  86, 140
Alexander, Harald  153, 165
Alexander, Sascha  19
Ampaw, King  107
Annaud, Jean-Jacques  107
Antel, Franz  75
Arend, Volker Maria  81

Ballmann, Herbert  2
Bannert, Walter  37, 59
Bartlett, Michael  84
Barylli, Gabriel  21
Baser, Tevfik  3, 165
Baumgärtner, Hajo  11
Bausch, Pina  82
Becker, Wolfgang  132
Behrend, Jens-Peter  104
Behrens, Alfred  167
Behrens, Gloria  19
Beiersdorf, Dagmar  138, 175
Belmont, Vera  126
Bender, Stephan  39
Berger, Helmut  33

Bierbichler, Josef 155
Billian, Hans 92
Birkin, Andrew 20
Blank, Richard 65
Blasberg, Frank Guido 27
Blumenberg, Hans-Christoph 72, 96, 141
Bockmayer, Walter 54
Boeck, Emanuel 30
Bogner, Franz Xaver 23
Bogner, Willy 45, 46
Bohm, Hark 65, 82, 179
Boldt, Rainer 56
Böll, Christoph 139
Bolzini, Adriano (=Robert McCahon) 142
Bondy, Luc 170
Brandauer, Klaus Maria 55
Brasch, Thomas 116
Bretzinger, Jürgen 130
Bringmann, Peter F. 5, 132
Brückner, Jutta 17
Buck, Detlev 39, 68
Bueb, Klaus 5
Bühler, Wolf-Eckart 6
Büld, Wolf 49
Bundschuh, Jörg 14
Buschmann, Christel 9, 13, 45

Carriere, Mathieu 184
Cavani, Liliana 49, 91
Celentano, Adriano 74
Chabrol, Claude 31, 145
Christallini, Giorgio 91
Claus, Richard 13, 81
Collector, Robert 122
Corti, Axel 170
Czenki, Margit 84

D'Anna, Claude 95
Dargay, Attila 175
Dawson, Anthony M. 26, 83

Dazzi, Tommaso 59
Denis, Claire 25, 130
Donner, Clive 3
Dorn, Dieter 44
Dörrie, Doris 54, 70, 98, 115
Draeger, Thomas 93
Dressler, Holm 182
Driver, Sara 140

Edel, Uli 92
Ehmck, Gustav 66, 137
Ehrhardt, Waltraud 78
Eichhorn, Christoph 74
Elci, Ismet 81
Emmerich, Roland 67, 104
Engel, Andi 51
Engström, Ingemo 47
Enyedi, Ildiko 101
Erler, Rainer 60, 108

Fellini, Federico 57
Fischerauer, Bernd 18
Fleischmann, Peter 40
Frank, Hubert 40, 87
Franke, Anja 33
Frankel, Cyril 50
Frankenberg, Pia 19, 109
Fratscher, Peter 7
Fröhlich, Klaudi 144
Funk, Dieter 123
Furtwängler, Florian 153
Fuster-Pardo, Rafael 72

Geissendörfer, Hans W. 21
Genee, Heidi 122
Gengnagel, Klaus 9
Gies, Hajo 181, 182
Gietinger, Klaus 133
Gilliam, Terry 2
Gisler, Marcel 131, 149

Glenn, Pierre-William  150
Glowna, Vadim  28
Glück, Wolfgang  4
Goedel, Peter  154
Goldschmidt, John  100
Gottlieb, Franz Josef  145, 182
Gottschalk, Thomas  182
Götz, Siggi  36, 144
Graef-Marino, Gustavo  146
Graf, Dominik  32, 78, 142, 151
Grandl, Peter  5
Graser, Jörg  3
Gregan, Ralf  101
Grosse, Nina  58
Gumm, Detlef  166, 183
Günay, Enis  161
Günther, Egon  125
Gutman, Nathaniel  168

Haffter, Petra  87
Hahn, Gerd  171
Hallervorden, Dieter  29, 101
Hamos, Gusztav  158
Hauff, Reinhard  16, 92, 144
Helfer, Daniel  123
Heller, Peter  20
Herbrich, Oliver  39
Herz, Juraj  53
Herzog, Werner  25
Hiemer, Leo  133
Hoffman, Jerzy  18
Hoffmann, Günter  143
Hofmann, Ilse  150
Hofmann, Nico  85, 89, 118
Hohlfeld, Horant H.  23
Horst, Hartmut  10
Hubert, Jean-Loup  85
Huettner, Ralf  47, 96
Huillet, Daniele  152
Huston, John  151

Imhoff, Markus 122
Iosseliani, Otar 158

Jahn, Hartmut 154
Janson, Uwe 162
Jordan, Murray 62
Juncker, Michael 168
Junker, Gottfried 164

Karo, Nikolai 77
Kaurismäki, Mika 64
Keglevic, Peter 96, 140
Kern, Peter 26, 61
Keusch, Erwin 46
Kiral, Erden 30
Klahn, Thees 112
Klein, Gerd 162
Klier, Michael 157
Klopfenstein, Clemens 95
Kluge, Alexander 7, 164
Knilli, Maria 48
Koeppe, Sigrus 109
Kollek, Amos 51
Koller, Xavier 135
Konermann, Lutz 135
König, Ulrich 63
Königstein, Horst 63
Konyar, Rasim 161
Kosmidis, Paris 73
Kotulla, Theodor 7
Krenkler, Ulrich 184
Krieger, Martin Theo 183
Kubny, Werner 98
Kückelmann, Norbert 137
Kühn, Kristian 146
Kurnitzky, Horst 109
Kürten, Berno 89
Küster, Diethard 161

Lähn, Michael 78
Lambert, Lothar 32, 138
Lang, Fritz 101
Lautenbacher, Klaus 44
Laux, Michael 123
Lelouch, Claude 93
Lemke, Klaus 15
Levy, Dani 33, 124
Lilienthal, Peter 121, 136
List, Niki 171
Livaneli, Zülfü 38
Loriot (= Vicco von Bülow) 111
Lottaz, Beat 123, 145
Lottmann, Eckart 10
Lübbert, Orlando 83
Ludman, Larry 127
Lukschy, Stefan 30
Luther, Slavo 155

Malle, Louis 10
Mansur, Fauzi 153
Marcello, Dieter 6
Margheriti, Antonio 141
Marian, Edwin 26
Masten, Werner 108, 130
Mather, Ted 27
Mattei, Marius 62
Mauch, Thomas 5, 99
McCahon, Robert (=Adriano Bolzini) 142
Meerapfel, Jeanine 86, 163
Menegoz, Robert 29
Menzel, Jiri 133
Mertner, Ingrid 107
Michael, Jörg 135
Michelberger, Erwin 85
Miehe, Ulf 159
Mikesch, Elfi 163
Miller, George 158
Milonako, Ilia 118, 134
Mittermayr, Berthold 36

Mordillat, Gerard 185
Moroder, Giorgio 101
Morrissey, Paul 14
Müller, Hanns Christian 97
Müllerschön, Nikolai 111, 112
Münster, Reinhard 4

Näter, Thorsten 147
Negri, Alberto 112
Nekes, Werner 76
Neumeier, John 77
Noever, Hans 48, 53, 93

Odermatt, Urs 54
Olsen, Rolf 144
Onneken, Edzard 36
Ottinger, Ulrike 75

Patzak, Peter 76, 79, 167
Paulus, Wolfram 63, 105
Perraudin, Rene 181
Petit, Christopher 24
Polak, Jindrich 115
Possardt, Werner 177
Pröttel, Dieter 55
Puhl, Reginald 129

Rademakers, Fons 125
Rateuke, Christian 29, 137
Retzer, Otto W. 144
Rey-Coquais, Cyrille 58
Rinaldi, Carlos 69
Ripploh, Frank 102, 150
Rödl, Josef 173
Rothemund, Sigi 15
Rudolph, Claude-Oliver 175
Rudolph, Verena 49
Runze, Ottokar 61

Sander, Helke 45
Sanders-Brahms, Helma 44, 90, 98
Schaack, Michael 171
Schaaf, Johannes 103
Schäfer, Dirk 170
Schamoni, Peter 24, 131
Schatzberg, Jerry 172
Schenkel, Carl 185
Schier, Heiko 169
Schilling, Niklaus 8
Schlicht, Burghard 133
Schlingensief, Christoph 29, 68, 156
Schlöndorff, Volker 11, 56, 152
Schmid, Marion 109
Schmidt, Eckhart 6, 172
Schott, Elld Antonio 182
Schrader, Uwe 139
Schröder, Claudia 41, 166
Schroeder, Barbet 142
Schroeter, Werner 126
Schuller, Frieder 71
Schütte, Jan 31, 173
Schwabenitzky, Reinhard 37, 41
Schwarzenberger, Xaver 15, 57, 113, 114
Seck, Amadou Saalum 129
Sempel, Peter 28
Senft, Haro 73
Serafini, Marco 136
Sharon, R. 83
Sigl, Robert 90
Silber, Rolf 144
Söth, Sandor 117
Speck, Wieland 171
Stadler, Heiner 81
Stark, Ulrich 14
Steiner, Rudolf 51, 159
Steinheimer, Gert 186
Stelly, Gisela 169
Stelzer, Manfred 24, 67
Sternberg, Raoul 86

Stöckling, Tania 58
Storch, Wenzel 58
Storch, Wolfgang 185
Straub, Jean-Marie 152
Strecker, Frank 8
Stripp, Peter 159
Suarez, Bobby A. 97
Syberberg, Hans Jürgen 105
Szabo, Istvan 62

Taviani, Paolo 106
Taviani, Vittorio 106
Tessari, Duccio 16
Thome, Rudolf 102, 117, 138, 149
Thorn, Jean-Pierre 69
Timm, Peter 46, 100
Tressler, Georg 147
Treut, Monika 76, 163
Tröster, Jürgen 172

Ullrich, Hans-Georg 166, 183
Ulmke, Heidi 132
Urchs, Wolfgang 71

Vajda, Marijan 113
Van Ackeren, Robert 162
van Beveren, Tim 74
Verhoeven, Michael 80, 134
Vesely, Herbert 117
Vilsmaier, Joseph 65
Vollmar, Wolf 43
von Bülow, Vicco (Loriot) 111
von Grote, Alexandra 110
von Lützelburg, Helmer 70
von Praunheim, Rosa 8, 157, 165
von Sydow, Rolf 80
von Theumer, Ernst Ritter 121
von Trotta, Margarethe 45, 52, 124, 127

Waalkes, Otto  113, 113, 114
Wächter, F. K.  79
Wagner, Christian  168
Wagner, Maria Teresia  105
Wargnier, Regis  50
Wawrzyn, Lienhard  56
Weiss, Jiri  100
Wember, Bernward  38
Wenders, Wim  66
Wesnigk, C. Cay  163
Wessel, Kai  99
Wichniarz, Karsten  17
Wicker, Wigbert  29, 106
Wicki, Bernhard  143
Wieland, Ute  70
Winkelmann, Adolf  116
Woernle, Bettina  35
Wolfsperger, Douglas  79, 90
Wolman, Dan  37

Young, Robert W.  7

Zanussi, Krzysztof  174
Zehetgruber, Rudolf  108
Ziedrich, Ecki  139
Ziewer, Christian  152
Zschokke, Matthias  35
Zurborn, Ernst-August  154
Zuta, Daniel  43

# INDEX OF ACTORS AND ACTRESSES

Names in parentheses indicate pseudonyms or real names, respectively. Spelling variations commonly used in German:

ä = ae; ö = oe; ü = ue; ß = ss.

Abel, Alfred  102
Abraham, F. Murray  108
Abt, Katharina  5
Achternbusch, Herbert  48, 64, 66, 103, 118, 174
Adams, Maud  121
Adorf, Mario  28, 103, 125
Affolter, Therese  84, 144
Afroni, Yehuda  37
Agbinowu, Emmanuel  107
Agenin, Beatrice  50
Aghfurian, Natascha  21
Ahrens, Thomas  92
Akina, Henry  84
Aksoy, Serap  38
Alexander, Jace  66
Allen, Karen  151
Allen, Terry  6
Almeida, Adelina  109
Altan, Ayse  4
Altaras, Adriana  72, 99, 102, 117, 138
Altmann, Michael  79
Altmanova, Jana  100
Alvarado, Angela  59
Alvarenga, Murilo  104
Ameise,  85
Ampaw, King  25

Anconina, Richard 94
Anders, Birgit 18, 117
Anders, Christian 145
Anderson, Andy 112
Anderson, John 6
Andor, Lotto 78
Andorai, Peter 101
Andre, Carola 62
Anholt, Christian 173
Anno, Kelby 46
Ansari, Nicole 150
Anzenhofer, Thomas 152
Aoyama, Mariko 82
Arantes, Romulo 121
Araoz, Elida 17
Arbas, Derya 30
Ardant, Fanny 52
Arikan, Jale 145, 161
Arndt, Adelheid 24, 63, 65
Ascopane, Dotsche 44
Ates, Seyran 85
Auer, Barbara 23, 45, 66, 162
Augustin, Gustl 67
Augustinski, Peer 32
Aziz, Rutkay 38

Babe, Fabienne 167
Bach, Dirk 70
Bach, Patrick 8
Backmann, Edda Heidrun 135
Badenhorst, Gesa 147
Badji, Saly 158
Badura, Gabriele 85
Baduri 32
Baes, Steve 143
Baeza, René 121
Baka, Miroslaw 157
Bakhayokho, Diankou 129
Balamir, Hakan 30
Balasis, Jorgos 164

Baldwin, Alec 52
Balke, Pago 68
Bär, Dietmar 98
Baratta, Martina 152
Baratta, Vladimir 152
Bardischewski, Leo 123
Bargeld, Blixa 28
Barner, Nora 123
Barnstedt, Imke 175
Baron, Yves 74
Barr, Robert 59
Barranco, Maria 184
Barrymore, Drew 3
Barth, Isolde 146
Barylli, Gabriel 21, 171
Basile, Salvatore 25
Bates, Alan 31
Bathke, Wolfgang 169
Battaglia, Guillermo 69
Baumgartner, Franz 48, 174
Baumgartner, Monika 24, 134
Baye, Nathalie 14
Beach, Roger 134
Beals, Jennifer 31
Becker (Nosbusch), Desiree 2
Becker, Meret 171
Becker, Rolf 18
Beck, Susanne 41
Beginnen, Ortrud 47
Behnke, Frank 39
Behpour, Delia 108
Behpour, Miriam 108
Behrend, Klaus 154
Behrends, Ela 138
Beilikke, Frank 124
Beilke-Lau, Ankie 61
Beilke, Ankie 9, 16
Belafonte, Shari 45
Belfari, Rosario 17
Belmondo, Jean-Paul 94

Beluch, Pjotr 27
Benati, Anne Marie 82
Bender, Dominik 99
Bender, Ostap, Jr. 39
Beneyton, Yves 87
Benn, Alex 16
Bennent, Heinz 71
Bennett, Hywel 169
Bennett, Steven 41
Bensasson, Lucia 109
Berger, Gunther 2, 13, 31, 81, 87
Berger, Helmut 2, 32, 58
Berger, Senta 80
Berger, Toni 63
Berger, Wilhelm 121, 149
Berger, Wolfram 54, 181
Berling, Peter 25
Bernardy, Desiree 92
Berndl, Christa 61
Berndt, Werner 163
Bernhard, Joachim 133
Bernhardt, Andreas 171
Bernhardt, Joachim 86
Bert, Alfred 40
Besoiu, Ion 71
Bestvater, Thomas 100
Betschart, Susanne 136
Beutler, Barbara 102
Bexter, Charles 40
Beyer, Susan 93
Bhasker 31
Biczycki, Jan 52
Biczycki, Jan-Paul 77, 127
Biedermann, Julia 137
Biedrzynska, Adriana 62
Bierbichler, Annamirl 64, 103, 106, 118, 174
Bierbichler, Annemarie 156
Bierbichler, Josef 156
Bierstedt, Marie 104
Birkin, Jane 14, 50

Bishop, Kelly 70
Blair, Linda 122
Blanc, Dominique 170
Blanco, José Maria 117
Blasen, Bernd 163
Blaszczyk, Ewa 133
Blech, Hans-Christian 4, 16
Blecker, Geraldine 132
Bliese, Joachim 80
Blum, Ina 8, 76
Blumberger, Erika 125
Blumensaat, Georg 114
Bockmeyer, Walter 70
Boehm, Franz 9, 168
Boehnicke, Lena 312
Böhm, Katharina 149
Bohm, David 65
Bohm, Hark 5, 39, 65, 82, 109, 113, 185
Bohm, Marquard 73
Bohm, Uwe 65, 179
Böhm-Wildner, Herta 106
Bohringer, Richard 85
Bois, Curt 67
Boisson, Christine 48
Boitano, Brian 23
Bokel, Radost 16, 103
Bolant, Roberto 153
Bonacelli, Paolo 50
Bonetti, Massimo 106
Boning, Wigald 63
Borgelt, Hans-Henning 56
Borgnine, Ernest 59
Boschan, Barbara 123
Böttcher, Enrico 96
Boyd, Karin 74
Boysen, Markus 122
Boysen, Rolf 44
Brammer, Philipp 143
Branchart, Gunhild 129
Brand, Marinus 177

Brandauer, Klaus Maria  20, 55, 62, 143
Brandis, Jonathan  158
Brandt, Volker  141
Brauer, Charles  9, 182, 185
Brauer, Tina  21
Braun, Heinz Josef  177
Brauner, Sharon  18
Brauren, Katharina  110, 111
Bredehöft, Susanne  29, 132
Breitner, Paul  87
Brejchova, Jana  53
Brem, Rudolf Waldemar  91
Brenes Calvo, Rolando  82
Brennan, Eileen  3
Brenner, Hans  24
Brescia, Mariano  103
Breuer, Jacques  23
Breuer, Marita  164
Brialy, Jean-Claude  130
Brice, Pierre  182
Brieger, Nicolas  171
Brolin, James  66
Brömse, Waggie  103
Brook, Irina  100
Brown, Victor  153
Bruckhorst, Natja  151
Buchfellner, Ursula  11
Buchholz, Christopher  130
Buchrieser, Franz  106, 140
Buck, Detlev  39, 68
Bucknor, Kofi Baba  5
Buder, Ernst-Erich  115
Bueb, Klaus  5, 109
Buhre, Traugott  173
Bulin, Franz  98
Burch, Jeannine  31
Burkhard, Gert  133
Burkhard, Ingrid  4
Burrasch, Monica  129
Burt, Clarissa  158

Buschhoff, Walter  117
Buschke, May  13
Bussotti, Fabio  50

Caceres Molina, Claudio  72
Calhoun, Monica  114
Canonica, Anni Sibylle  108, 168
Cantieni, Ursula  118
Capraru, Jennifer  167
Capucine  17
Carallo, Antonio  82
Cardinahl, Jessika  113
Cardoso, David  153
Carlisle, Anne  66
Caroll, Helena  151
Carriere, Matthieu  14, 18, 75
Carstens, Christiane  123, 132
Carstensen, Margit  68
Carter, Helena Bonham  50
Caspar, Eric P.  60
Cassens, Dagmar  36
Castaldi, Jean-Pierre  64
Caster, Conrad  91
Cat, Fritz the  53
Cave, Nick  28
Celentano, Adriano  74
Celi, Adolfo  142
Cetinkaya, Baris  161
Cetinkaya, Yavuzer  38
Cevio, Marc  123
Chaffee, Suzy  46
Chaliapin, Feodor, Jr.  107
Chalupa, Vaclav  100
Chen, Steven  140
Choucou, Adam  130
Christensen, Ute  115
Cieslinski, Peter  162, 164
Circe  134
Cisse, Binta  158
Clarke, Margi  64

Clement, Aurore  35
Clevenot, Philippe  69
Clever, Edith  105
Cluzet, Francois  25
Coen, Aram  89
Colli, Mathias  156
Collins, Lewis  26, 83
Coltrane, Robbie  24
Connelly, Christopher  127
Connery, Sean  107
Conrad, William  80
Constantine, Eddie  41
Cordova, Eliana  83
Corley, Al  6, 63
Cotta, Stephanie  146
Coy, Jonathan  100
Craig, Michael  142
Craigie, Ingrid  151
Cramer, Susanne  69
Crecelius, Janos  141
Creip, Monic  5
Cremer, Ute  152
Cronjäger, Nina  5
Crosby, Mary  75
Cuny, Alain  170
Curtis, Kelly  97
Curtis, Tony  116
Cutini, Mario  134
Czach, Etta  86
Czerwinski, Barbara  172
Czypionka, Hansa  142

d'Angelo, Mirella  27
Daevers, Madeleine  167
Dali, Candice  121
Dall, Karl  138
Daman, Gabriel  151
Danon, Geraldine  53
Dautzenberg, Dirk  2
Davis, Brad  125

Dawson, Anthony 26, 142
Day, Sushila 84
de Ahna, Kerstin 143
de Bankole, Isaach 25, 130
de Grazia, Julio 16
de Luda, April 112
de Mendoza, Alberto 69
de Paris, Zazie 13
de Rossi, Barbara 59, 146
Dedem, Daniel 136
Dee, Georgette 163
Degen, Elisabeth 83
Degen, Michael 83
Deisen, Dagmar 73
Deisinger, Lutz 149
Delany, Cathleen 151
Delorme, Danièle 110
Demarmels, Claudia 139
Demirkan, Renan 182
Denalane, Sarah Jane 74
Dennehy, Brian 55
Dentler, Markus 30
Descas, Alex 130
Deschauer, Luise 91
Desny, Ivan 112
Dette, Kai 11
Deutschmann, Heikko 99, 167
Dick, Michael 162
Dicken, Dieter 165
Dickow, Hans-Halmut 172
Diess, Karl-Heinz 43
Diess, Karl-Walter 136
Dietl, Harald 3, 43
Diffring, Anton 167
Diop, Abdoul Azis 129
Disse, Iris 146
Disselkamp, Sascha 131
Djadjam, Mostefa 126
Dobra, Anica 142
Dobra, Anna 125

Dobrin, Emilia 71
Dobson, Peter 92
Doermer, Christian 155
Doll, Birgitt 16, 109
Dommartin, Solveig 67, 69, 130
Donadio, Cristina 83
Donatz, Esther 118
Donovan, Stacey 92
Donutil, Miroslav 53
Dorff, Thomas 78
Dornblut, Sabine 9
Draeger, Jürgen 6
Drechsler, Petra 62
Dresewski, Brigitta 147
Drocar, Jakub 115
Ducasse, Cecile 25
Duerr, Hans Peter 183
Duessler, Robert 99
Dumont, Sky 113
Dunaway, Faye 20, 56
Dunne, Griffin 70
Dünßer, Crescentia 168
Durning, Charles 152
Dury, Ian 20
Dutronc, Jacques 143
Duvall, Robert 56
Duvier, Angelique 26
Duwner, Gert 108
Dux, Ferdinand 98
Dylong, Grazyna 161
Dymna, Anna 18
Dziallas, Wilfried 147

Eaves, John 46
Eberth, Claus 106
Eberts, David 20
Echerer, Mercedes 105
Edel, Alfred 14, 29, 39, 68, 99, 103, 109, 112, 156, 181
Eichenseher, Mark 131
Eichhorn, Christoph 54, 87

Eichhorn, Lisa 104
Eklund, Tina 119
Elci, Ismet 82
Elsner, Hannelore 4, 16, 78, 154
Eltes, Polly 132
Elwes, Cary 100
Emirli, Ilhan 179
Emo, Maria 57
Engel, Marlies 18
Engel, Tobias 4, 58
Engelbrecht, Constanze 139
Engelbrecht, Nadja 100
Engelsing, Tobias 91
Engin, Sema 167
Eperjes, Karoly 62, 90
Erikci, Mahmet 30
Eschke, Elfi 38
Evans, Michelle 30
Eyison, Joe 107

Faber, Heike 123
Fabian, Francoise 173
Fabrizi, Franco 57
Fairchild, Morgan 80
Falk, Peter 67
Fallenstein, Karina 9, 29, 71
Fani, Eleonora 62
Färber, Helmut 81
Faverey, Anette 67
Fecht, Özay 10, 165
Fechter, Anna 156
Fedder, Jan 139
Fehrmann, Helma 33, 38
Feik, Eberhard 8, 118, 150, 181, 182
Fejtö, Raphael 10
Feldmann, Rötger "Brösel" 171
Felhio, Fabienne Joelle 129
Fellensiek, Uwe 81, 175
Felsenheimer, Dirk 124
Felton, Martine 175

Fenner, Barbara 26
Ferch, Heino 169
Ferrera, Stephane 87
Fiedler, Bea 37
Filipenko, Alexander 40
Film, Agnes 58
Finch, Jon 117, 146
Finck, Wolfgang 147
Finckh, Beate 16, 78
Firchow, Reinhard 48
Fischer, Angela 78
Fischer, Gabi 177
Fischer, Helmut 144, 182, 182
Fischer, Irene 156
Fischer, Joschka 161
Fischer, Vera 153
Fleischmann, Nele 169
Fletcher, Suzanne 140
Flex, Judith 163
Flimm, Jürgen 35
Fonda, Peter 126
Forbes, Gary 19
Forbes, Martin 19
Forsyth, Tony 63
Fortell, Albert 17, 109, 145
Foster, Hugh 75
Fötzinger, Erich 62
Franca, Marlene 153
Frank, Jeffrey 18
Franke, Anja 33, 124
Franke, Peter 132, 152
Frankenberg, Pia 20, 109
Franz, Birgit 47
Freer, Laila Florentine 155
Freitag, Benedict 159
Frey, Sami 90, 127
Freyse, Gunter 64, 118
Fricke, Peter 41
Fricsay, Andras 7, 123, 138, 139
Friedrich, Karl 46

Froboess, Cornelia 44, 141
Fröhlich, Gustav 102
Früh, Giovanni 147
Frühwald, Arnold 96
Fullerton, Fiona 50
Fux, Herbert 14, 62

Gabriel, Gudrun 168
Gahr, Michael 134, 143
Gainsbourg, Charlotte 106
Galler, Waltraud 64
Gander, Richard 79, 91
Ganz, Bruno 67
Garbers, Gerhard 20
Garbo, Frank 5
Garcin, Stéphane 110
Garner, Christine 80
Gaspar, Dominique 76
Gautier, Anne 40
Gautier, Susanne 32
Gebel, Malgoscha 39, 102
Gedeck, Martina 123, 151
Geer, Andy 14
Geerken, Hartmut 48
Geerken, Sigrid 48
Geißler, Margit 29, 77
Geist, Gabi 48, 64, 118, 174
Gelin, Daniel 80, 94
George, Clayton 184
George, Götz 16, 78, 150, 181, 182
George, Heinrich 102
Gertsch, Max 27
Gertz, Jami 185
Gertzen, Hubertus 184
Ghazala, Amira 183
Ghirardelli, Claudia 103
Gholmie, Riad 132
Giggenbach, Robert 134
Gillich, Hans Peter 135
Gilot, Yolande 2, 150, 185

Girotti, Massimo 91
Glass, Ann Gisel 139
Glatzeder, Winfried 161
Gleason, Paul 67
Glenn, Julie 151
Gnädinger, Mathias 54, 173
Gökgöl, Demir 165
Goldberg, Michael 71
Golden, Annie 52
Golino, Valeria 52
Gomez, Carlos 27
Gomez, Yvonne 23
Gorges, Ingolf 138
Goschi, Giulia 25
Gossett, Louis, Jr. 11
Gostischa, Theo 9, 89
Gottschalk, Thomas 16, 36, 50, 182, 182
Gould, Elliott 76
Graefe, Katharina 136
Grafl, Hans 79, 91
Grams, Rene 100
Granger, Stewart 121
Grassmann, Werner 81
Grau, Hans Joachim 85
Graudus, Konstantin 98
Greene, Ellen 70
Grefa, Edica 159
Greiling, Michael 57
Grenkowitz, Rainer 100, 106
Griem, Helmut 24, 44
Griyp, Mia 43
Groetschel, Inka 92
Grossmann, Mechthild 82, 163
Groth, Sylvester 103
Grube, Michael 183
Grünberg, Klaus 9, 100
Grünmandl, Otto 65
Gueye, Awa Cheickh 129
Guhlich, Volker 51
Guiomar, Julien 5

Gurnett, Jane 51
Guth, Klaus 41
Gutzwiller, Isabelle 6
Güzelce, Talcin 166
Gwisdek, Michael 66, 82

Haack, Christina 27
Haag, Romy 112
Haas, Ludwig 26
Haber, Alessandro 153
Habich, Matthias 116
Hackl, Karl-Heinz 171
Hagen, Eva Marie 169
Hagen, Nina 28
Haider, Alfons 62
Hajdu, Vladimir 155
Halldorsdottir, Kolbrun 135
Haller, Isa 97
Hallervorden, Dieter 15, 29, 41, 101
Hallwachs, Hans Peter 24, 29, 89, 113, 141, 158, 168
Hallyday, Johnny 151
Halmer, Günter-Maria 3, 80, 105, 111
Hamann, Evelyn 111
Hambitzer, Heinrich 153
Hamel, Lambert 7, 21
Hamerstein, Dominik 183
Hamilton, Chico 97
Hamilton, Suzanna 28, 146
Hammer, Sascha 171
Häni, Gaston 133
Hardie, Kate 51
Harfouch, Corinna 82
Harlander, Willy 125
Harmstorf, Raimund 23, 55
Harnisch, Wolf 60
Harry, Debbie 52
Hartmann, Maria 58
Hasenäcker, Maria 165
Hatheyer, Heidemarie 99
Haußmann, Ezard 15

Haucke, Gert  29
Hauff, Alexander  100
Havers, Nigel  146
Haydee, Marcia  77
Hedl, Kio Cornel  59
Heimberg, Liliana  136
Heinrich, Klaus  109
Heins, Albert  138, 175
Helfrich, Uwe  132
Helm, Brigitte  102
Hemminger, Hansjörg  109
Hennemann, Sabine  163
Hentz, Mike A.  158
Herbst, Norman  51
Herder, Andreas  131
Herkenrath, Bernward  58
Herletz, Susanne  106
Hermann, Irm  75
Herrschmann, Johannes  99, 117, 138
Herz, Gabriele  45
Herzog, Werner  54
Heyer, Ursula  31, 101
Hibbert, Jennifer  20
Hickey, William  107
Hielscher, Liane  9
Hilb, Liora  6
Hildebrandt, Dieter  97
Hill, Angie  30
Hirsch, Antje  172
Hoenig, Heinz  4, 21, 46, 50, 78, 146
Hoesl, Tobias  93
Hofer, Herbert  119
Höfferer, Sissy  26
Hoffman, Dustin  152
Hoffmann, Jutta  7
Hofmann, Josef  124
Hofschneider, René  27
Hoger, Nina  139
Höhn, Carla  131
Höhne, Jürgen  58

Holzmann, Thomas 43
Honesseau, Mikael 8
Hoppe, Marianne 131
Hoppe, Rolf 80
Hörmann, Annette 63
Horn, Camilla 131, 159
Hornett, Gillian Tuyudee 6
Hornung, Matheiu 149
Horwitz, Dominique 46, 99
Hosang, Andreas 68
Hosen, Tote 49
Hrusinsky, Jan, Jr. 53
Hube, Jörg 24, 38, 155
Huber, Grischa 83
Huber, Lotti 8, 86, 158
Hubert, Antoine 85
Hubert, Julien 85
Hübner, Kurt 126
Hübner, Roger 169
Hülsmann, Ingo 73
Hunger, Angela 110
Hunter, Holly 11
Hurley, Elizabeth 140
Huston, Anjelica 151
Hutton, Lauren 17

Idle, Eric 2
Idler, Rolf 134
Illig, Rolf 168
Iskandarani, Mustafa 175

Jaenicke, Anja 114, 124, 130
Jaenicke, Hannes 66, 111, 123, 181
Janda, Krystyna 90
Jankowiak, Günther 38
Jankowski, Oleg 101
Janner, Brigitte 3, 61
Jansen, Corinna 135
Jantimatorn, Surachai 6
Javaronne, Franco 59

Jecklin, Ruth 137
Jecloos, Johannes 5
Jefford, Barbara 173
Jelmini, Tiziana 59
Jendreyko, Hans-Dieter 95
Jensen, Beate 24, 87, 146
Jesserer, Gertraud 5
Jimenez, Luz 121
Jitreekan, Arunotai 54
John, Gottfried 24, 133
Johns, Alexandra 158
Jonasson, Andrea 143
Jones, Freddie 100
Josephson, Erland 62
Juhnke, Harald 61
Jung, Andre 164
Junge, Katja 99
Jürgens, Jenny 91

Kaack, Sabine 151
Kafka, Tamara 102
Kaiser, Dorothea 89
Kaiser, Ingrid 35
Kalan, Yavuz 161
Kammer, Heinz 158
Kammer, Joachim 142
Kantemir (Family) 86
Karlowa, Elma 168
Karlsdottir, Hanna Maria 135
Karmalker, Ravi 78
Karner, Brigitte 90
Karven, Ursula 17, 172
Katay, Endre 90
Katzur, Jesse 37
Kaufmann, Christine 40, 57, 112, 114
Kaufmann, Günter 172
Kausch, Brigitte 29, 68
Kaven, Wolfgang 98
Keller, Marthe 75, 126
Kelling, Sissy 49

Kelterborn, Klaus 18
Kemmer, Joachim 78, 130, 171
Kempe, Harald 169
Kenda, Roland 186
Kensit, Patsy 140
Kent, Julia 80, 86, 97
Kern, Peter 75, 85, 173
Kernen, Siegfried 46, 73
Kesten, Christian 165
Keziban, Alisan 82
Kiel, Sue 122
Kieling, Wolfgang 29, 60
Kier, Udo 158, 163
Kilbinger, Hans-Gerd 74
Kinalzik, Ulli 108
Kinski, Klaus 25, 83, 142
Kinski, Nastassja 106
Kinski, Pola 84
Kirchberger, Sonja 139, 162
Kirchgässner, Erika 85
Kirchhoff, Corinna 122, 143
Kirchlechner, Dieter 77
Kish, Laszlo I. 123
Kiss-Tamas, Laslo 117
Kistner, Andy 15
Klaffenböck, Rudi 156
Klaus, Francois 77
Klein, Gad 76
Klein-Rogge, Rudolf 102
Kleiner, Towje 53, 136
Kleinert, Volkmar 113
Klöppel, Jutta 138
Klos, Vladimir 77
Klubowicz, Marta 157
Knaak, Anne 131, 145
Knaup, Herbert 168
Knebel, Gerd 132
Knie, Rolf 133
Knops, Detlev 59
Koch, Uwe-Karsten 74

Kogelnik, Petra 37
Kollhoff, Heiner 85, 186
Konarek, Ernst 186
Koneczny, Boris 125
Konermann, Lutz 135
König, Michael 7, 48, 73
Königer, Miklos 84
Kontic, Ljijala 164
Kopfmüller, Mathias 85
Körner, Diana 112
Körning, Jörg 167
Körösi, Csaba 71
Kosmalla, Jessica 133
Kotzur, Sabine 104
Kovacevic, Sami 51
Krabbe, Jeroen 51
Kraeft, Volkert 15
Kraehkamp, Heinz 79
Kranz, George 97
Kraupa, Arpad 71
Kraus, Peter 96, 141
Krause, Erna 86
Krause, Michael 157
Krawinkel, Gert "Kralle" 32
Kreindl, Werner 36, 133
Kremer, Anette 72, 144
Krenner, Heidrun 135
Kretschmer, Cleo 70, 139
Kreuzer, Lisa 146
Kreye, Walter 154
Krieg, Christopher 156
Krieger, Gerard 39
Krieger, Ulrike 19
Kriener, Ulrike 47, 55, 98
Kristel, Sylvia 121
Krol, Joachim 174
Krueger, Jan 183
Krug, Manfred 108, 172
Krüger, Chantalle 40
Krüger, Mike 36, 55, 138

Krüger, Pit 61
Krumbiegel, Werner 165
Kruse, Anja 36
Kuckuck, Henner 93
Kuhlbrodt, Dietrich 68
Kuiper, Peter 113
Kukavica, Nascica 19
Kulenkampff, Hans-Joachim 144
Kuno, Stefan 36
Kunze, Andreas 76
Kurtiz, Tuncel 10, 61
Kurz, Bruno 109
Kurz, Eva 165
Kusdas, Ulf Dieter 36
Kusuhara, Eiji 16
Kutlucan, Hussi 170
Kutschke, Marion 8
Kviring, Ivo 84
Kwabena, Osei 107

L., Marie-Sophie 94
Lacey, Deborah 5
Lackmann, Gottfried 54
Laforet, Marie 185
Laimböck, Adolf 89, 162, 186
Laisakul, Paijong 6
Lambert, Lothar 82, 175
Lamla, Norbert 184
Lamm, Regina 17
Lampe, Jutta 170
Lamprecht, Günter 18, 126
Landers, Audrey 75
Landgrebe, Gudrun 66, 71, 78, 91
Landovsky, Pavel 48
Landuris, Dieter 92
Lang, Stephan 92, 152
Längsfeld, Wolfgang 81
Lansink, Leonard 67, 81, 139
Lareti, Käbi 47
Lato, Danuta 45

Lauffen, Richard 111
Lause, Hermann 116, 141, 169
Lautenbacher, Klaus 44
Lauterbach, Heiner 5, 19, 26, 80, 98, 115
Lauterburg, Christine 95
Lavie, Amos 169
Lavy, Pascal 154
Le Doyen, Laurent 35
Le Vaillant, Nigel 55
Leaud, Jean Pierre 43, 112
Lebenheim, Eva 93
Leder, Erwin 36
Ledl, Lotte 4
Lee, Dexter 140
Lee, Mark 109
Lehmann, Katharina 179
Lehmann, Manfred 26, 83, 127, 136
Lehnert, Tillmann 8
Leiberg, Angela 56
Leigh, Jennifer Jason 92
Leipnitz, Harald 182
Leipzig, Dina 59, 149
Lemberger, Monika 103
Lerman, Hans 56
Leroy, Philippe 141
Leslie, John 19
Levy, Dani 33
Lewanowski, Ilona 10, 56, 184
Lewgoy, José 25
Leysen, Johan 95
Lhermitte, Thierry 185
Liebold, Sissi 37
Lieffen, Karl 107
Liegl, Edgar 156
Lind, Jakov 136
Lindig, Julia 170
Lingenberg, Darja 183
Link, Steve 46
Liska, Ivan 77
Lissa, Eva 49

Lively, Jason 67
Lohmeyer, Gero 47
Lohmeyer, Peter 108, 142
Lonsdale, Michael 107
Lopez Vasquez, Luis 53
Lopez, Maria Isabel 97
Loriot (= Vicco von Bülow) 111
Lösch, Andrea 141
Lonsdale, Michael 96
Lot, Michael 99
Lother, Susanne 173
Lowell, Carey 70
Löwitsch, Klaus 78, 141
Lozano, Margarita 106
Lucas, Andy 171
Lucas, Drew 86
Luchette, Veriano 95
Lück, Ingolf 49, 116
Ludwig, Anna 98
Ludwig, Bernd 145
Lünenschloß, Vera 77
Lüönd, Walo 41
Lütkens, Horst 147
Lütge, Martin 13, 82

MacDowell, Malcolm 104
Macherron, Calvin 84
Mächlinger, Otto 135
Maffay, Peter 76
Magnuson, Ann 140
Mahler, Norbert 47
Maldonado, Javier 121
Malkovich, John 152
Malkowski, Alexander 102
Malvoy, Christophe 50
Manesse, Gaspard 10
Manfredi, Nino 64
Manfredi, Robert 64
Manker, Paulus 39, 101
Manopas, Sira 109

Manowski, Beatrice  117
Manzke, Bernd  51
Marangosoff, Janna  98
Maranow, Maja  41, 165
Marcan, Jacqueline  119
Marcus, Edgar  163
Mareck, Heinz  50
Margulies, David  97
Marian, Edwin  75
Marischa, Juliette  14
Marius, Robert  97
Marschall, Marita  154, 169
Martin, Remi  155
Martin, Sonja  37, 117
Martinek, Julia  144
Martini, Louise  110
Marwitz, Michael  184
Marx, Horst-Günther  162, 164
Masina, Giulietta  57
Maslo, Karl  132
Mastroianni, Marcello  57
Mathe, Gabor  101
Matheis, Ilse  79
Matic, Peter  167
Matschoss, Ulrich  99, 150
Matschulla, Claudia  117
Mattes, Eva  9, 38, 45, 65
May, Alexander  15
May, Barbara  47, 113
May, Gisela  61
May, Martin  47
Mayer, Ilona  65
Mazer, Emilia  16
McCann, Donald  151
McCarthy, Andrew  146
McDaniel, Tim  67
McGee, Jack  97
McGovern, Elizabeth  56
McLaughlin, Sheila  163
McNally, Kevin  91

Mehner, Alexander  122
Meier, Dieter  28, 184
Meier, Heinz  181
Meinecke, Katharina  89
Meinke, Stefan  80
Meisner, Günter  54
Melba-Fendel, Heike  76
Melikyan, Krikar  112
Mell, Marisa  62
Melles, Sunnyi  4, 9, 32, 44, 55, 100, 115, 173
Menez, Bernard  29
Messner, Claudia  57, 137, 171, 181
Messner, Reinhold  109
Meurer, Herbert  153
Meyer-Brockmann, Frank  49
Meyer-Kohlhoff, Stephan  43
Meyer, Sabine  58
Mich, Brybida  27
Michael, Wolfgang  35
Mikolajczak (= Miko), Petra  102
Miller, Rebecca  55
Millet, Christiane  110
Milva  174
Mira, Brigitte  136
Mitchum, Bentley  59
Mitchum, Chris  59
Mnouchkine, Alexandere  127
Monn, Ursela  55, 110, 137
Montezuma, Magdalena  126
Moog, Heinz  155
Moore, Geoffrey  45
Moore, Natalie  40
Moore, Roger  45
Moorse, Ian  9
Moosbrugger, Christoph  41
Moravsky, Tanja  15
Morawiecz, Barbara  138
Morena, Lolita  31
Morgenstern, Ralf  54
Mori, Claudia  75

Morier-Genoud, Philippe 10
Morita, Pat 3
Moritz, Dorothea 79
Moro, Federica 75
Morrison, Kenny 158
Mueller-Stahl, Armin 7, 48, 76, 80, 103, 137, 143, 159
Mueller-Stahl, Hagen 136
Mühe, Ulrich 143
Müller-Westernhagen, Marius 96, 132
Müller, Hans-Reinhard 134
Müller, Richy 125, 146, 175
Mulligan, Richard 3
Munoz, Margarita 17
Münster, Klaus 136
Muntean, Remus 9
Murray, Jane 129
Muzzulini, Muzzu 145
Myers, Kitty 109

Nadler, Rudolf 131, 149
Nägel, Franz 74
Nardulli, Itaco 141
Naszinski, Lara 155
Naumann, Holde 36
Naumann, Jens 33
Navarrete, Roberto 121
Neff, Dorothea 49
Negret, Francois 10
Neitzel, Edith 154
Nelson, Craig T. 70
Nembi, Olivier 85
Nena 159
Nero, Franco 7, 59
Neubauer, Christina 150
Neubauer, Ilse 8
Neville, John 2
Nico 13
Nicoel, Cristus 119
Niehoff, Domenica 150
Niendorf, Horst 108

Niesner, Timmo 86
Niklas, Jan 31, 126
Nikolakakis, Nektaria 164
Nitzsche, Ella 39
Nortey, Grace 107
Notthoff, Günter 18
Nowack, Romina 47
Nowald, Thomas 144
Noy, Zachi 37, 145
Nucci, Leo 95
Nygren, Mia 117

Oates, Simon 30
Oberholz, Dieter 132
Obermeir, Daniela 105
Obernigg, Martin 20
Ochsenknecht, Uwe 21, 30, 45, 55, 98, 111, 123, 146
Ofoe, Grace 107
Ogier, Bulle 143, 170
Ohno, Kazuo 28
Okay, Yaman 161, 165
Okten, Göler 30
Olafsdottir, Ruth 3
Olbrychski, Daniel 124
Olcay, Zuhal 3
Olin, Lena 47
Oliver, Jill 92
Olivera, Oswaldo 158
Ollrogge, Ingrid 38
Olschewski, Gerhard 110, 118
Orbach, Jerry 92
Orcier, Sylvie 58
Ordonez, Eva 96
Orfgen, Samy 54
Orlando, Antonio 126
Orser, Brian 23
Orth, Elisabeth 55
Osburg, Gabriele 110
Ossenkopp, Barbara 163
Ostermayer, Christiane 73

Ostrander, William  122

Padilla, Samuel Caento  159
Page, Ilse  84
Pajanou, Despina  15
Pajor, Tamas  117
Palance, Jack  114
Palo, Jukka-Pekka  47
Paradise, Sal  172
Pare, Michael  104
Pascalin, Oliver  53
Pastewka, Anna  157
Patton, Will  1, 24
Paul, Adrian  27
Paulus, Albert  64, 105
Paulus, Joanna  105
Pauly, Rebecca  116
Paurat, Leonore  44
Pavlidis, Carlos  177
Pawalek, Klaus  85
Payre, Bruce  185
Pedersen, Gudjon  135
Pekny, Romuald  44
Pektidou, Nikos  164
Peppard, George  185
Pepper, Jeanny  92
Perrier, Mireille  25
Perryment, Mandy  50
Pesce, Dante  121
Pestalozzi, Adriane  36
Peterson, Jan  8
Petit, Pascale  7
Petri, Elke  109
Petri, Marcella  134
Petsch, Stefanie  172
Pfaff, Dieter  15
Pfennigwerth, Jörg  13
Piccoli, Michel  100, 170
Piele, Alexander  93
Pinnow, Horst  124

Pinon, Dominique 28
Pirchner, Florian 64
Pistor, Ludger 171
Plate, Christina 138
Pleasance, Donald 26, 127
Pleitgen, Ulrich 4, 144
Pleva, Jörg 60
Plewka, Jan 21
Plimpton, Martha 185
Pochath, Werner 91, 97
Pochert, Gabi 123
Poderosi, Augusto 57
Pohland, Britta 108, 118
Poiret, Jean 139
Polt, Gerhard 97
Pounder, CCH 114
Poysti, Tom 47
Pradal, Bruno 110
Praetorius, Karl-Friedrich 86
Prati, Pamela 97, 147
Preen, Zak 102
Prieto, Aurore 69
Princigali, Guia 103
Princigalli, Giacomo 103
Prinz, Dietmar 14
Prochnow, Jürgen 28, 80, 140, 151
Provenza, Sal 93,
Prückner, Tilo 61, 162
Pryce, Jonathan 2
Przygodda, Peter 81
Pszoniak, Wojtek 141

Quadflieg, Will 122
Quest, Hans 24
Quester, Hugues 40
Quinn, Aidan 56
Quinn, Anthony 141
Quinn, Daniel 27

Raab, Kurt 123, 143, 154, 174

Raacke, Dominic  15, 47
Raake, Catarina  123
Rabal, Francisco  59
Rabau, Erika  32
Racette, Francine  10
Rachmann, Sigurd  171
Radzun, Alexander  82
Rames, Samuel  95
Ramm, Gerhard  39
Ramon, Lila  40
Ramras, Len  136
Raschen, Kristina  124
Raspe, Margarete  138
Rattinger, Anton  36
Rau, Lieselotte  89
Rauch, Sibylle  19, 38, 172
Rauch, Siegfried  145
Rauter, Knut  184
Reed, Oliver  2
Reed, Sarah Polley  2
Reents, Claus-Dieter  35, 161
Reeves, Keanu  3
Regent, Benoit  31
Regnier, Carola  163
Regnier, Charles  116
Rehberg, Michael  7, 137
Reichardt, Elke  145
Reichel, Achim  161
Reichmann, Wolfgang  14, 60
Reid, Kate  152
Reidenbach, Felix  169
Reincke, Heinz  107
Reindl, Sigmund  14
Reinhold, Judge  125
Reinthaller, Ulrich  48
Reiser, Rio  134
Relton, Linda  153
Remmler, Stephan  32
Renzi, Eva  142
Rettenwender, Gerta  64

Retzer, Otto  23
Richardson, John  62
Richardson, Natasha  56
Richter, Ilja  11
Richter, Ingrid  62
Richter, Ralf  78
Richter, Ralph  175
Ripploh, Frank  102, 150
Rippy, Leon  104
Riva, Manuela  132
Rivera, Marie Elena  17
Robakiewicz, Maciej  174
Robards, Jason  173
Robin, Michael  57
Roderer, Walter  31, 137
Roggisch, Peter  7, 73
Rohrbeck, Oliver  53, 108
Rohrmoser, Klaus  113
Rois, Sophie  68
Rökk, Marika  131
Roland, R.  73
Römer, Anneliese  73
Romey, Ayse  179
Rönnefarth, Burkhard  172
Rosa, Robby  59
Rosenberg, Marianne  84
Roth, Eva  20
Roth, Wolf  74
Rourke, Mickey  50
Roussel, Myriem  162
Rübling, Steffen  18
Rud, Bernard  43
Rüdlinger, Max  95
Rudnik, Barbara  159
Rudolph, Claude Oliver  6, 7, 65, 81, 122
Rudszun, Alexander  78
Rufus  182
Rühaak, Simen  159
Rupe, Katja  159
Russek, Rita  139

Rutherford, Karleen 33

S., Ulrike  82
Sachers, Walter  6
Sadoyan, Isabelle  85
Sägebrecht, Marianne  26, 100, 114, 125
Sagna, Moussa  158
Sagna, Sigalon  158
Sahin, Necati  163
Saint-Macavy, Marc  131
Samel, Udo  152
Sander, Otto  67, 124, 167, 181
Sander, Ute  114
Sanders, George  142
Sandrelli, Stefania  127
Sands, Julian  106, 174
Sastre, Ines  75
Sattmann, Peter  57, 74
Saygili, Mustafa  72
Scacchi, Greta  52
Scalici, Gillian  75
Schade, Doris  124
Schalaudeck, Alexandra  89
Schanelec, Angela  152
Scharf, Alfons  156
Schech, Michael  170
Schediwy, Fritz  35
Schell, Maximilian  126
Schellschmidt, Ilja  56
Schenk, Otto  145
Schenk, Udo  26, 57, 150
Schiff, Peter  101
Schildkraut, Eric  99
Schindler, Michaela  135
Schindler, Rotraud  101
Schirm, Ulrike  138
Schlechter, Thomas  170
Schlicht, Burghard  134
Schmahl, Hildegard  169
Schmid-Burgk, Angela  169

Schmidinger, Dolores 7
Schmidinger, Walter 24
Schmidt, Andreas 145
Schmidt, Antje 15
Schmidt, Peer 136
Schmidtchen, Kurt 93
Schmücke, Thomas 146
Schnaubelt, Alexandra 138
Schneeberger, Gisela 97
Schneider, Helge 76
Schnelling, Otto 13
Schödl, Hans 86
Schoenaerts, Julien 43
Schoenau, Marlies 183
Scholz, Roy 144
Schönfelder, Friedrich 114
Schönherr, Dietmar 5, 152
Schötz, Daniela 3
Schrader, Inga 32
Schrader, Maria 124
Schroeder, Jochen 137
Schroth, Hannelore 65, 168
Schubert, Heinz 41
Schubert, Karin 19
Schücke, Thomas 185
Schuh, W. L. 93
Schühly, Nina 150
Schulenberg, Maria 129
Schultz, Ilona 92, 166
Schultz, Nina 10
Schumacher, Wolfgang 18
Schumann, Erik 143
Schündler, Rudolf 9
Schunke, Thomas 59
Schütter, Friedrich 26
Schwartz, Alexandra 58
Schwarzmaier, Michael 63
Schweiger, Heinrich 96
Schygulla, Hanna 3, 52
Scott, Colleen 77

Seck, Elhdaj Abdoulaye 129
Segal, Jonathan 37
Segda, Dorota 101
Seibt, Tatja 167
Seidel, Silvia 8
Seidl, Rupert 96, 177
Seiler, Elisabeth 136
Seipold, Manfred 97
Seippel, Edda 111
Seitz, Franz 81
Selge, Edgar 133
Sen, Füsun 161, 179
Seneca, Joe 11
Serbedzija, Rade 164
Serre, Henri 69
Sevenich, Anke 57, 154
Seweryn, Andrzej 50
Sexpert, Susie 76
Seyhun, Deniz 10
Seyrig, Delphine 75
Shelton, Deborah 182
Shopp, Nicolas 165
Silberschneider, Johannes 171
Simanek, Otto 115
Simonischek, Peter 52, 147
Singer, Maria 3
Sinjen, Sabine 24
Slater, Christian 107
Slims, Tom 46
Söderbaum, Krista 91
Sola, Michel Angel 16
Sommer, Elke 67, 145
Sommerfeld, Nirit 170
Son, Kali 138, 139
Soral, Agnes 80
Soutendijk, Renee 43, 96, 174
Spanou, Dimitra 164
Speck, Wieland 82
Spengler, Volker 29, 68, 116
Sperr, Martin 24

Spielberg, Thomas  73
Spizzico, Gianvito  103
Spoerri, Miriam  35
Spohn, Philip  144
Sprenger, Wolf-Dietrich  31, 89, 118, 173
Sprotelli, Andreas  86
Stahl, Susanne  138
Stallone, Frank  80
Stalone, Teli  134
Stangl, I.  171
Steeger, Ingrid  7
Steiger, Renate  135
Steinbeck, Jan  63
Steiner, John  26, 83, 127
Steiner, Sigfrit  93
Steinmetz, Eric  102
Stepanek, Cordula  131
Sterr, Michelle  36
Stewart, Alexandra  116
Stewart, Sally  27
Stingl, Kiev  13
Stocker, Werner  9, 65
Stokowski, Oliver  130, 151
Stolze, Lena  134
Storch, Wenzel  58
Strätz, Ursula  173
Straub, Jean J.  18
Straub, Laurens  48
Strecker, Rainer  171
Strempel, David  183
Studt, Katja  21
Sukowa, Barbara  124, 127, 164
Surgere, Helene  69
Suske, Stefan  137
Symo, Margit  26
Szapolowska, Grazyna  62, 140
Szinetar, Dora  90

Tai, Ling  134
Taifun, Nilgün  32

Takaki, Mio  91
Takayama, Noguyuki  85
Tanir, Macide  38
Tauber, Bernd  21, 123
Tavernier, Nils  139
Tegtmeyer, Anke  71
Teixeira, Virgilio  143
Temessy, Heidi  90
Temrite-Wadzatse, Agnelo  104
Temucin, Maric  72
Tennant, Victoria  184
Terzieff, Laurent  126
Testi, Fabio  112
Teutscher, Pauline  134
Tez, Melek  86
Thalbach, Katharina  4, 47, 48, 115, 116, 181
Thanheiser, Johannes  39
Thomas, Angelika  99
Thomas, Heather  145
Thomas, Terry  62
Thompson, Brian  104
Tiefenbach, Matthias  131
Tiefenbacher, Friederike  117
Tiller, Nadja  141
Tin Hong, Che  95
Tjan, Willy  78
Tobias, Oliver  75, 127
Todd, Tony  140
Tomelty, Frances  20
Tonkel, Jürgen  36
Torn, Rip  185
Tornade, Pierre  29
Traier, Dieter  146
Traub, Marianne  76
Trieste, Leopoldo  103
Trintignant, Jean-Louis  50
Trixner, Heinz  4
Trooger, Sabine  9, 164
Trunz, Frank  165
Tschechowa, Vera  39, 149

Tschiersch, Jockel 36
Tukur, Ulrich 13, 45, 45, 45, 45, 72, 144
Türgay, Niyazi 86
Tushingham, Rita 63
Twerenbold, Hans Rudolf 95

Uhlen, Anette 45
Uhlen, Susanne 133
Uhlig, Gerald 154
Ullissner, Thomas 165
Ullmann, Liv 126
Umbach, Martin 158
Uriona, Marcelo 61, 76
Uttler, Claudia 143
Uzzaman, Buddy 31

Väänänen, Kari 64
Valandrey, Charlotte 126, 185
Valdivielso, Maru 155
Valentin, Barbara 55, 70
van Bergen, Ingrid 35, 74, 124
van Cleef, Lee 26
van Eyck, Kristina 87
van Houhuys, Heinz 81
van Lyck, Henry 63
Vavrova, Dana 65, 115
Vernon, Howard 152
Verrett, Shirley 95
Vetchy, Ondrej 100
Vetter, Jan 124
Viet , Hans E.68
Vivas, Victoria 40
Vlady, Marina 48
Vlasak, Jan 115
Vogel, Helmut 64
Vogel, Jürgen 21, 77, 81, 110, 125, 175
Vogel, Nikolaus 15
Vogler, Karl Michael 104
Vogler, Rüdiger 39, 149, 155
Volker, Klaus 35

Volkmann, Elisabeth  54, 122
Volter, Philippe  95
von Arnim, Piero  53
von Borsody, Suzanne  46
von Boxberg, Bertram  132
von Dobschütz, Ulrich  141
von Friedl, Loni  16
von Ledebur, Friedrich  57
von Lersner, Brigitte  93
von Liebezeit, Karl-Heinz  89
von Manteuffel, Felix  111
von Maydell, Sabine  5, 175
von Praunheim, Rosa  165
von Quast, Nini  106
von Rauch, Andreas  152
von Reichlin, Fee  131
von Ruffin, Kurt  158
von Strombeck, Peter  6, 112
von Thun, Friedrich  17, 168
von Togni, Olga  49
von Weitershausen, Gila  18
Voß, Andy  147
Vrzal-Wiegand, Ivo  173

Waalkes, Otto  113, 113, 114
Wagner, Vanessa  139
Wahl, Emel  15
Wahl, Wolfgang  146
Walken, Christopher  169
Walsh, Tahne  76
Walter, Kristina  139
Wameling, Gerd  109
Wandel, Rüdiger  57
Wanitschek, Heinz  132
Warens, Guntbert  166
Waterston, Sam  28
Weber, Bernhard  72
Wedekind, Claudia  108
Wegner, Sabine  144, 164
Weigl, Vladimir  102, 136

Weinzierl, Kurt 36
Weisberger, Eleonore 184
Welper, Sven 131
Wenders, Wim 81
Wennemann, Klaus 108, 159
Wepper, Elmar 23
Werner, Ilse 61, 72
Werner, Marcel 13
Wessely, Rudolf 48
West, Samuel 173
Westheimer, Ruth 52
Whitlow, Jill 67
Wichmann, Joachim 186
Wicki, Bernhard 80
Widmark, Richard 11
Wiedemann, Elisabeth 113
Wieder, Hanne 115
Wiegandt, Mine-Marei 173
Wilcek, Raphael 136
Wildgruber, Ulrich 31, 51
Willer, Isabelle 111
Williams, Ron 20, 87, 144
Willman, Ralph 153
Wilson, Ajita 119
Wilson, Lambert 126
Wilson, Stuart 184
Wink, Jürgen 117
Winkler, Ralph 129
Winkler, Thomas 151
Winslow, Michael 182, 182
Winter, Birgit 5
Wismuth, Franz 9
Witt, Katarina 23
Wolff, Susanne 131
Wolff, Veronika 184
Wollner, Gerhard 29
Wollter, Sven 154
Wolter, Ralf 32
Wood, Stefan 96
Wosien, Bernhard 49

Wrzesinski, Michael  51
Wülfing, Silke  9
Würzbach, Dolly  49
Wussow, Klaus-Jürgen  16, 107

Yandirer, Mechmet  26
Yanne, Jean  185
Yesilkaya, Hayati  99
Yieser, Petra  92
Yontan, Gürel  38
York, Michael  76, 80
York, Susannah  51
Young, Burt  92
Young, Dey  182
Young, Ric  31

Zacher, Rolf  24, 64, 116, 137, 141, 146, 162, 181
Zadok, Arnon  169
Zadora, Pia  49
Zafer, Ylmaz  30
Zaluski, Renee  83
Zapatka, Manfred  43
Zebrowski, Josef  157
Zech, Rosel  7, 15, 65, 164
Zentara, Edward  40
Zerlett, Wolfgang  113
Zierl, Helmut  139
Zimmerling, Robert  110
Zimmerscheid, Siegfried  67, 173
Zirner, August  9, 23, 45, 55
Zischler, Hanns  31, 50, 67, 91, 149, 155, 162
Zivojinovic, Beta  164
Zöckler, Billie  15, 55, 70
Zsoldos, Valeria  117
Zündel, Elisabeth  99, 138

# CROSS-REFERENCE INDEX OF ENGLISH TITLES

(Original English titles, proper names, numbers, etc. used as titles are not included here. Check German film listings.)


*A Chick for Cairo*   *Küken für Kairo*
*A Circus Full of Adventure*   *Ein Zirkus voller Abenteuer*
*A Gathering of Old Men*   *Ein Aufstand alter Männer*
*A Guru is Coming*   *Ein Guru kommt*
*A Journey to Germany*   *Eine Reise nach Deutschland*
*A Little Happiness*   *Das einfache Glück*
*A Meeting with Rimbaud*   *Ein Treffen mit Rimbaud*
*A Swiss Named Nötzli*   *Ein Schweizer namens Nötzli*
*A Tooth for a Tooth*   *Zahn um Zahn*
*A Virus has no Morals*   *Ein Virus kennt keine Moral*
*Abraham's Gold*   *Abrahams Gold*
*Accomplices*   *Komplizinnen*
*Adrian and the Romans*   *Adrian und die Römer*
*AIDS - The Coming Danger*   *AIDS - Die schleichende Gefahr*
*Ain't Nothin' Without You*   *Nicht nichts ohne dich*
*All Hell's Breaking Loose in Heaven*   *Im Himmel ist die Hölle
    los*
*Alphacity*   *Alphacity - Abgerechnet wird nachts*
*And the Same to You*   *Du mich auch*
*And There Was Light*   *Und es ward Licht*
*Anita - Dances of Vice*   *Anita - Tänze des Lasters*
*Autumn Milk*   *Herbstmilch*
*Awakenings*   *Aufbrüche*

*Babes in Toyland*   *Abenteuer im Spielzeugland*
*Bagdad Cafe*   *Out of Rosenheim*
*Banana Paul*   *Bananen Paul*

249

*Bang! You're Dead! (The Microchip Killer)* Peng! Du bist
    tot!
*Beyond Blue* Jenseits von Blau
*Bibo's Men* Bibo's Männer
*Big Mac* Big Mäc
*Black and without Sugar* Schwarz und ohne Zucker
*Blood and Honor - Youth in Hitler's Realm* Blut & Ehre -
    Jugend unter Hitler
*Blue Moon - Breathless through the Night* Blue Moon - Atemlos
    durch die Nacht
*Blue-eyed* Blauäugig
*Boomerang - Boomerang* Bumerang - Bumerang
*Boran - Time to Aim* Der Fall Boran
*Bread and Butter* Butterbrot
*Bride of the Orient* Gekauftes Glück
*Burning Beds* Brennende Betten
*Burning Secret* Brennendes Geheimnis
*Butterflies* Schmetterlinge

*C\*A\*S\*H - A Political Fairy-Tale* Schweinegeld - Ein Märchen der
    Gebrüder Nimm
*Caspar David Friedrich - Limits of Time* Caspar David Friedrich -
    Grenzen der Zeit
*Castle Königswald* Schloß Königswald
*Children of Stone* Kinder aus Stein
*Chocolate - Forbidden Desires* Chocolat - Verbotene Sehnsucht
*Cocaine: The Diary of Inga L.* Kokain - Das Tagebuch der
    Inga L.
*Concert for the Right Hand* Konzert für die rechte Hand
*Crazy Times* Starke Zeiten

*Days to Remember* Die Verliebten
*Death of a Salesman* Tod eines Handlungsreisenden
*Death of a White Horse* Der Tod des weißen Pferdes
*Devil's Paradise* Des Teufels Paradies
*Didi Drives Me Crazy* Didi auf vollen Touren
*Didi Times Seven* Didi und die Rache der Enterbten
*Double* Doppelgänger
*Dragon's Food* Drachenfutter
*Duel* Zweikampf

e.g. ... *Otto Spalt*    z.B. ... *Otto Spalt*
*Earthbound*    *Erdenschwer*
*Edvige Scimitt - A Life between Love and Insanity*    *Edvige Scimitt -*
    *Ein Leben zwischen Liebe und Wahnsinn*
*Electro-Paralysis - A Movie Against Powerlessness*    *Elektro-*
    *Lähmung - Ein Film gegen die Ohnmacht*
*Empedocles' Death*    *Der Tod des Empedokles*
*Escape to the North*    *Flucht in den Norden*
*Ether Delirium*    *Ätherrausch*
*Europe, At Dusk*    *Europa, abends*

*Farewell to a False Paradise*    *Abschied vom falschen Paradies*
*Feel the Motion*    *Der Formel Eins Film*
*Fire, Ice and Dynamite*    *Feuer, Eis & Dynamit*
*Fire and Ice*    *Feuer und Eis*
*First the Work, and Then What?*    *Erst die Arbeit und dann?*
*Five Beers and a Coffee*    *Fünf Bier und ein Kaffee*
*Föhn Researchers*    *Die Föhnforscher*
*Fool's Mate*    *Zugzwang*
*For Ever and Ever*    *Auf immer und ewig*
*Forbidden Dreams*    *Verbotene Träume*
*Forever, Lulu*    *für immer: Lulu*
*Forget It*    *Vergessen Sie's*
*Forty Square Meters of Germany*    *40 qm Deutschland*
*Four Men and a Camel*    *Nägel mit Köpfen (Vier Männer und*
    *ein Kamel)*
*From the Gutter to the Stars*    *Miko - Aus der Gosse zu den*
    *Sternen*
*Fucking Fernand*    *Zwei halbe Helden*

*Gamblers*    *Spieler*
*Gas for the Kids*    *Sprit für Spatzen*
*Geierwally*    *Die Geierwally*
*Georg Elser, One Man from Germany*    *Georg Elser - Einer aus*
    *Deutschland*
*Georgette*    *Die Gottesanbeterin*
*German spoken Here*    *Man spricht deutsch*
*Ginger and Fred*    *Ginger und Fred*
*Girls' Favorite Sport*    *André schafft sie alle*
*Good-bye Children*    *Auf Wiedersehen, Kinder*

*Gravel    Kies*

*Handsome    Der Schönste*
*Hard to Be a God    Es ist nicht leicht ein Gott zu sein*
*Harry and Harriet    Eine Frau namens Harry*
*He and I    Ich und Er*
*Heal Hitler!    Heilt Hitler!*
*Heart with a Spoon    Herz mit Löffel*
*Hello and Welcome    Herzlich willkommen*
*Hidden Love    Versteckte Liebe*
*Holiday    Ausgeträumt*
*How Loyal is Nik?    Wie treu ist Nik?*
*Hunter of Angels    Jäger der Engel*

*I Only Have Your Love    Hab ich nur Deine Liebe*
*I Want to Live with You    Ich möchte mit dir leben*
*Ice    Eis*
*If I Only Have Your Love    Hab' ich nur deine Liebe*
*I'm Your Slave    Ich bin dir verfallen*
*In My Heart, Darling    In meinem Herzen, Schatz*
*In the Desert    In der Wüste*
*In the South of my Soul    Im Süden meiner Seele*
*In the Year of the Turtle    Im Jahr der Schildkröte*
*Iron Earth - Copper Sky    Eisenerde - Kupferhimmel*

*Jacob Behind the Blue Door    Jacob hinter der blauen Tür*
*Jannan - the Deportation    Jannan - die Abschiebung*
*Joan Lui    Joan Lui*
*Johann Strauss - King without a Crown    Johann Strauss - Der König
         ohne Krone*
*Josefine Mutzenbacher's Love Academy      Die Liebesschule der
         Josefine Mutzenbacher*
*Jungle Mission    Unser Mann im Dschungel*

*Kiebich and Dutz    Kiebich und Dutz*
*King Kong's Fist    King Kongs Faust*
*Kiss of The Tiger    Der Kuß des Tigers*
*Kunyonga - Murder in Africa    Kunyonga - Mord in Afrika*

*Land in Sight    Land in Sicht*

*Land of the Fathers, Land of the Sons    Land der Väter, Land der Söhne*

*Last Exit Brooklyn    Letzte Ausfahrt Brooklyn*

*Lemon Popsicle VI: Vacation Romance    Eis am Stiel 6. Teil - Ferienliebe*

*Lemon Popsicle VII: Boys in Love    Eis am Stiel, 7. Teil - Verliebte Jungs*

*Lemon Popsicle VIII: West of Eden    Eis am Stiel, 8. Teil - Summertime Blues*

*Line 1    Linie 1*

*Lisa and the Giants    Lisa und die Riesen*

*Live and Die Wild    Lebe kreuz und sterbe quer*

*Lock and Seal    Schloß und Siegel*

*Lovable Zanies    Zärtliche Chaoten*

*Love and Fear    Fürchten und lieben*

*Loyal Johann    Der treue Johannes*

*Lucky Galoshes    Galöschen des Glücks*


*Macao - or The Back Side of the Sea    Macao oder Die Rückseite des Meeres*

*Maneuvers    Manöver*

*Martha and Me    Martha und ich*

*May Storms    Gewitter im Mai*

*Melancholia    Der fünfte Freitag*

*Men    Männer*

*Mixed News    Vermischte Nachrichten*

*Money    Geld*

*Moon Hunters    Mondjäger*

*My God, Didi!    Mein Gott, Didi!*

*My Twentieth Century    Mein 20. Jahrhundert*

*My Father's War    Der Krieg meines Vaters*


*Nessie, the Craziest Monster in the World    Nessie, das verrückteste Monster der Welt*

*Niemann's Time    Niemanns Zeit*

*Night Sun    Nachtsonne*

*1938: Home to the Realm    '38 - Heim ins Reich*

*Nötzli Twice    Der doppelte Nötzli*

*Nonstop Troubles with The Experts    Der Experte*

*Nose Dive    Sturzflug*
*November Cats    Novemberkatzen*
*November Moon    Novembermond*

*Oh Rosa!    Winckelmanns Reisen*
*On a Roll    Voll auf der Rolle*
*One Hundred Years of Adolf Hitler - The Last Hours in the*
        *Führer's Bunker    Hundert Jahre Adolf Hitler — Die letzte*
        *Stunde im Führerbunker*
*One Look and it's Love    Ein Blick und die Liebe bricht aus*
*Operation Madonna    Der Madonna-Mann*
*Orchids of Insanity    Orchideen des Wahnsinns*
*Orgy of Death    Orgie des Todes*
*Ossegg or the Truth about Hansel and Gretel    Ossegg oder Die*
        *Wahrheit über Hänsel und Gretel*
*Otto out of Frisia    Otto - Der Außerfriesische*
*Otto - The Movie    Otto - Der Film*
*Otto - The New Movie    Otto - Der neue Film*

*Pan Tau - the Movie    Pan Tau - der Film*
*Paradise    Paradies*
*Paths Pursued    Verfolgte Wege*
*Perils of Love - AIDS    Gefahr für die Liebe - AIDS*
*Pestalozzi's Mountain    Pestalozzis Berg*
*Peter in Wonderland    Peter im Wunderland*
*Please Let the Flowers Live    Bitte laßt die Blumen leben*

*Quiet Days in Clichy    Stille Tage in Clichy*

*Real Men Don't Eat Gummy Bears    Gummibärchen küßt man*
        *nicht*
*Red Heat    Red Heat - Unschuld hinter Gittern*
*Red Kisses    Rote Küsse*
*Red Roses for a Callgirl    Manila Tatoo*
*Richard & Cosima    Wahnfried - Richard & Cosima*
*Room 36    Zimmer 36*
*Ruth    Blutiger Schnee (zu Freiwild verdammt)*

*School Girls - Ready for Love    Schulmädchen - Reif für die*
        *Liebe*

*Seduction: The Cruel Woman*      *Verführung: Die grausame*
        *Frau*
*Seven Women    Sieben Frauen*
*Shadow of the Desert    Schatten der Wüste*
*Silence like Glass    Zwei Frauen*
*Sissi - The Movie    Sissi - der Film*
*Sleepy Betrayers    Stille Betrüger*
*Soldier Boys on the Loose    Die Küken kommen*
*Something's Fishy on the Ark    In der Arche ist der Wurm  drin*
*Special Command Force Wild Geese    Spezialkommando Wildgänse*
*Survival in New York    Überleben in New York*

*Taxi to Cairo    Taxi nach Kairo*
*The Accomplice    Der Einbruch*
*The Adventures of Baron Munchhausen        Die Abenteuer des*
        *Baron Münchhausen*
*The Attack    Der Angriff*
*The Berlin Affair    Leidenschaften*
*The Bicyclist from San Christobal        Der Radfahrer vom San*
        *Christobal*
*The Black Forester    Der schwarze Tanner*
*The Camelia Lady    Die Kameliendame*
*The Camera Man    Der Kameramann*
*The Cat    Die Katze*
*The Chinese are Coming    Die Chinesen kommen*
*The Chocolate Sniffers    Die Schokoladen-Schnüffler*
*The City Pirates    Die Stadtpiraten*
*The Colony    Die Kolonie*
*The Colors of the Indios    Die Farbe der Indios*
*The Curse    Der Fluch*
*The Days of the Birchboy    Die Zeit des Birkenjungen*
*The Dead    The Dead - Die Toten*
*The Death Brigade    Die Todesbrigade*
*The Eighth Day    Der achte Tag*
*The Exchange    Der Tausch*
*The Gamblers    Die Spieler*
*The Gatecrashers    Die Einsteiger*
*The German Chain Saw Massacre        Das deutsche Ketten-*
        *sägenmassaker*
*The Girl with the Cigarette Lighters        Das Mädchen mit den*

*Feuerzeugen*
The Glass Sky     *Der gläserne Himmel*
The Glider     *Der Flieger*
The Good Old Days     *Schön war die Zeit*
The Grass is Greener Everywhere Else     *Überall ist es besser, wo wir nicht sind*
The Green Hell of Cartagena     *Grüne Hölle von Cartagena*
The Greenhouse     *Das Treibhaus*
The Handmaid's Tale     *Die Geschichte der Dienerin*
The Hello Sisters     *Die Hallo-Sisters*
The Invincible     *Der Unbesiegbare*
The Invisible     *Der Unsichtbare*
The Joker     *Der Joker*
The Journey     *Die Reise*
The Little Attorney     *Der kleine Staatsanwalt*
The Man with the Trees     *Der Mann mit den Bäumen*
The Microscope     *Das Mikroskop*
The Name of the Rose     *Der Name der Rose*
The Nasty Girl     *Das schreckliche Mädchen*
The Neverending Story II     *Die unendliche Geschichte II - Auf der Suche nach Phantasien*
The Next Guy will be Different     *Beim nächsten Mann wird alles anders*
The Night of the Marten     *Die Nacht des Marders*
The Night     *Die Nacht*
The Officer Factory     *Fabrik der Offiziere*
The Philosopher     *Der Philosoph*
The Present attacks the Rest of Time     *Der Angriff der Gegenwart auf die übrige Zeit*
The Purloined Letter     *Der entwendete Brief*
The Queen's Complaint     *Die Klage der Kaiserin*
The Re-Found Friend     *Der wiedergefundene Freund*
The Return     *Die Rückkehr*
The Return of the Wild Geese     *Die Rückkehr der Wildgänse*
The Rose Garden     *Der Rosengarten*
The Rose War     *Der Rosenkrieg*
The Sexth Sense     *Der sexte Sinn*
The Skipper     *Der Skipper*
The Snowman     *Der Schneemann*
The Spider's Web     *Das Spinnennetz*

*The Spirit    Der Atem*
*The Splendor of These Days    Der Glanz dieser Tage*
*The Stone of Death    Der Stein des Todes*
*The Story Teller    Der Geschichtenerzähler*
*The Summer of the Falcon    Der Sommer des Falken*
*The Summer of the Samurai    Der Sommer des Samurai*
*The Turkish Spice Lady is Leaving    Die Kümmeltürkin geht*
*The Two Faces of January    Die zwei Gesichter des Januar*
*The Vast Land    Das weite Land*
*The Victor's Spoils or The Battle for the Stomachs of the World*
*        Das Brot des Siegers oder Die Schlacht um die Mägen der*
*        Welt*
*The Virgin Machine    Die Jungfrauenmaschine*
*The Voice    Die Stimme*
*The White-Collar Black Economy        Schwarzer Lohn und weisse*
*        Weste*
*The White Dwarfs    Die weißen Zwerge*
*The Wild Clown    Der wilde Clown*
*The Wings of the Night    Die Flügel der Nacht*
*The Wolf's Bride    Die Wolfsbraut*
*The Woman of my Dreams    Die Frau meines Lebens*
*The World Record    Der Rekord*
*The Writer's Silence    Das Schweigen des Dichters*
*Three against Three    Drei gegen drei - The Trio Film*
*Three Crazy Jerks    Zärtliche Chaoten 2*
*Tiger, Lion, Panther    Tiger, Löwe, Panther*
*Totally Crazy    Total bescheuert*
*Transitional Dreams    Transitträume*
*Triumph of the Just    Triumph der Gerechten*
*Tunguska - The Cartons are Here    Tunguska - Die Kisten sind da*

*Vatanyolu - The Voyage Home    Vatanyolu - Die Heimreise*
*Venus Trap    Die Venusfalle*
*Video Pirate    Der Videopirat*

*Waiting for Marie    Warten auf Marie*
*Waller's Last Trip    Wallers letzter Gang*
*War Zone - Death Zone    War Zone - Todeszone*
*Wedding    Wedding*
*Werner    Werner - Beinhart!*

*Westerners    Westler*
*When, if not Now?    Wann, wenn nicht jetzt?*
*Where To?    Wohin?*
*Wherever You Are    Wo immer du bist*
*Wings of Desire    Der Himmel über Berlin*

*You Elvis - Me Monroe    Du Elvis - Ich Monroe*
*Your Money or your Liver    Geld oder Leber*

# ABOUT THE AUTHORS

RICHARD C. HELT (Ph. D., Washington University, St. Louis) is Professor and Coordinator of German at Northern Arizona University. He has published *West German Cinema since 1945: A Reference Handbook* (Scarecrow, 1987) and other books and articles on German literature, German cinema, and German and American popular culture.

MARIE E. HELT (M.A.,University of Arizona) is Instructor of German at Northern Arizona University. She is co-author of *West German Cinema since 1945: A Reference Handbook* (Scarecrow, 1987). She has translated poetry from German to English and has published on German teaching methodology.